Thinking of...

Applying for a Patent in Australia?

Ask the Smart Questions

By Matt Lohmeyer and
Philip Heuzenroeder

Smart Questions™ Philosophy

Smart Questions is built on 4 key pillars, which set it apart from other publishers:

1. *Smart people want Smart Questions not Dumb Answers*
2. *Domain experts are often excluded from authorship, so we are making writing a book simple and painless*
3. *The community has a great deal to contribute to enhance the content*
4. *We donate a percentage of revenue to a charity voted for by the authors and community. It is great marketing, but it is also the right thing to do*

www.Smart-Questions.com

Reviews

"For any individual or small business considering filing an Australian patent application, investing the time to read Thinking of Applying for a Patent in Australia? *is an investment that will pay dividends."*

Yasmin King, Inaugural NSW Small Business Commissioner

"Applying for a patent in Australia *brings a new level of clarity to the question 'to patent or not to patent?'. Many Australian Organisations are not intimately aware of the power that intangible assets can provide them in the global marketplace. This book provides a fantastic first port of call for those pondering this question, and will provide insight into the key questions that need to be considered."*

Marcus Tarrant, Managing Director, Mission HQ Pty Ltd

"An enjoyable romp through the normally dry landscape of patenting! The book should be required reading for budding inventors."

Andrew Baker, Partner, GBS Venture Partners

"Most engineers and scientists would agree that the difference between success and failure in technical matters is usually the time taken to honestly answer a few smart questions. IP protection and commercialisation is no different. This book takes the masses of information available on the patent system and distils it into a simple, concrete methodology for evaluating and protecting any new idea. Matt and Philip have done a fantastic job in creating a useful tool for people of all levels of experience who want to make smart decisions about patent protection."

Warwick Bagnall, Chief Engineer, Cavitus Pty Ltd

"This book is exactly what we need. Hopefully it will encourage many inventors to 'unlock the bottom drawer' and let their inventions and IP take a breath of life. The approach is engaging and intelligent and will assist many entrepreneurs and angel investors to navigate the complexities of IP."

Christine Kaine, Founder, Business Angels Pty Ltd

"I wish I had read this book before I engaged an IP lawyer, I could have saved thousands in legal fees by being better prepared. Money which would have been better spent on marketing."

Jonathan Weinberg, Serial Entrepreneur and Owner, HeartCall Pty Ltd

"Thinking of Applying for a Patent in Australia? *answers all the questions you already have, and a few more you didn't know to ask, about this daunting process. I would make this required reading for anyone that asks about what to do with their invention. Well done to Matt and Philip for finally clearing the air on this tricky issue."*

Dr David Andrews, technology commercialisation executive

"If you are looking to patent, reading Smart Questions will improve your chances of getting a return on your investment."

David Mitchell, Chief Executive Officer, X-Energy Pty Ltd

"The Smart Question structure works extremely well. The authors have successfully consolidated their considerable personal experiences of IP and commercialisation to produce an exceptionally effective and useful tool for the reader."

David Cosgrave, Lecturer, The College of Law

"There are any number of publications available providing the fine detail on every aspect of patenting and IP due diligence. As an investor in early stage technology companies, I have struggled to find an IP user's guide that tells me what I want to know quickly and in a form that is easy to understand. Lohmeyer and Heuzenroeder's new book will make a great reference text or can be used as a comprehensive introduction for those wanting a broad understanding of the IP landscape in Australia."

Mark Bonnar, Investment Director, Cleantech Ventures Pty Ltd

Authors

Matt Lohmeyer, PhD

Matt is an independent consultant, helping inventors and businesses to protect and exploit their IP. After a 17-year career in drug development and technology commercialisation in the UK and Australia, Matt now manages his own business (*www.ip-resources.com*) and consults for Streamwise, a consulting firm specialising in business strategy and organisational development. As a trained negotiator and mediator, Matt assists industry and government clients with important commercial negotiations. He also teaches executive programs in advanced negotiation skills for Scotwork and is part of the adjunct faculty of the AGSM. Matt is married, has three children and a Labrador and hopes to succeed in negotiating access to the sofa and the TV remote some time soon.

Philip Heuzenroeder

Philip is a specialist intellectual property lawyer and a Principal at leading Australian IP firm Spruson & Ferguson (*www.sprusons.com.au*). He has nearly 20 years of legal and commercial experience, both in private practice and as in-house counsel, providing advice to clients in the energy, life sciences, ICT and other technology intensive industries. Philip works with clients ranging from individual inventors and SMEs through to major Australian universities, government departments and multi-nationals. He led the team that developed the IP Manual for Australian Government Agencies, as well as being a principal author of IP management handbooks prepared by Spruson & Ferguson with peak industry associations in the electrical, biotechnology and engineering fields. Philip is regularly asked to present workshops on issues relating to intellectual property in Australia and overseas. He is married with three children, all of whom have a sound grounding in copyright law...

Table of Contents

Acknowledgements

There is no shortage of detailed IP Manuals and expert books on intellectual property[1]. However, many of these books tend to be technical, highly detailed and exhaustive documents. Books full of answers – not everyone's cup of tea. For many years, we wished that someone would write a handy and pragmatic, 'user's guide' to patents and trade marks. A book to help inventors, scientists and entrepreneurs make better decisions about their own ideas. We envisaged a book without jargon, that doesn't seek to explain all the nuances of the law, but instead challenges its readers to think about the many diverse legal, commercial and personal issues involved in protecting and exploiting their IP.

A chance meeting with Stephen Parker of Smart Questions Limited ignited our passion to make this happen and made us realise that that elusive someone might as well be us. So the first thank you goes to Stephen, without whom this book might never have been started.

We also owe a lot of thanks to all our colleagues and mentors, past and present, from whom we have learnt so much over the years. Although we may not have always appreciated it at the time, the practical experience we have gained from observing and learning from their approach to practical problems, their successes, and of course occasional mistakes have been invaluable. Of course, the benefit of their experience and helpful guidance when a few of our own 'learning experiences' came back to haunt us also did not go astray.

We are grateful to all who have reviewed the book and provided candid feedback, helpful suggestions and their real world insights.

Most of all, we would like to thank the mainly unsung heroes for whom this book was written: the creative geniuses, inventors, entrepreneurs and scientists, without whom this world would be duller and poorer place. The patent system was created for you, and without you there would be no need for this book.

This is our chance to thank you for your contribution.

---

[1] For details of some of the books and manuals we recommend for further reading, see 'Sources of Further Information' at the back of the book.

The final thank you goes to our families and friends, who have endured evenings, nights and weekends of physical and mental 'absenteeism' on our part. In particular:

Donna, Tasch, Katya and Nick

Fenella, Ollie, Audrey and Mr P

We promise not to do it again (much) after we've finished the Smart Questions book on trade marks next year...

Foreword

Small Business is time poor, a fact that no small business owner will deny. In a society of ever increasing information overload, smart sources of information that provide a simple guide to complex concepts are as rare as a paperless office!

Thinking of … Applying for a Patent in Australia? is one of these rare finds. Written for inventors, entrepreneurs and small businesses, it provides a succinct self-help guide on how to make the most of innovative ideas, ensuring that they are able to be supported and protected under the Australian patent system.

Within the first few chapters of this book, the authors identify some of the key benefits of owning a patent but equally outline that obtaining a granted patent is not a cheap or easy process. For small businesses, which tend to have limited cash resources, wise decision-making is imperative, especially in the early stages of protecting any innovation.

The book's question and answer structure allows the reader to assess rapidly whether patenting is appropriate to their current needs and then guides the reader step by step through the process. It empowers inventors to become informed customers of professional intellectual property services and to use such services efficiently and effectively.

While small businesses face many challenges in terms of time and resources, they still must take the time to understand and be responsible for their longer-term competitive business interests. The responsibility to look after intellectual property should not be abdicated due to lack of knowledge.

For any individual or small business considering filing an Australian patent application, investing the time to read *Thinking of … Applying for a Patent in Australia?* is an investment that will pay dividends.

Yasmin King, BEc Hons, MBA, FCPA, FAICD

Inaugural NSW Small Business Commissioner

Who should read this book?

Anyone who wants to ensure that bright new ideas can become successful.

Generally, it is the creators of great new ideas that are most motivated to make them successful. The problem is that coming up with an invention and protecting, marketing and commercialising it are very, very different skillsets. If you have an inventive streak, are never quite satisfied with the way things are and constantly looking for ways to improve the world around you, then read on. This book is written principally for you. It is not technical and we have tried to steer clear of the jargon and legal mumbo-jumbo that often surrounds Intellectual Property (we'll call it 'IP' from now on to keep it simple).

This book is intended to be a catalyst and a guide for anyone dealing with novel ideas, inventions and new technologies in the context of a commercial enterprise. It is aimed squarely at those who see IP as something that should be utilised to serve business and society as a whole. Below are just a few examples of the kind of people who will find that this book may come in handy. Which one are you?

Inventors, Entrepreneurs & Researchers

Innovation and bright ideas are what drive and excite you. The grey suits looking after the commercial and legal aspects do not. This book will give you a toolbox of Smart Questions to ask. You can use these to challenge yourself and to keep your advisors on their toes. Addressing the Smart Questions will ease the long and sometimes tedious process of engaging with the commercial and

legal realities. Most importantly, knowledge and smart preparation will save you money and stack the odds of a successful outcome in your favour.

Business Owners

If you own a business that doesn't utilise IP, you probably haven't looked carefully enough! Can some of the innovative ways in which you run your business be protected and exploited? Have you or your staff developed patentable technologies that could be useful to others? Who owns them? How do you decide whether it's worth going to the trouble of protecting it? You need answers, but you need the answers that are right for *your* business. The kinds of answers that only come from asking Smart Questions.

Directors & CEOs of Technology Companies

You are in charge of an SME with an existing and expanding IP portfolio – and the costs of maintaining that portfolio. The patent attorneys and the research team seem determined to protect everything, but does everything need protection? How do you sort the wheat from the chaff? Can you contain costs without affecting future opportunity? Learning to ask Smart Questions will help you to get to the core of what's important and pave the way to a decisive and rational outcome for the business.

Angels & Venture Investors

You've been offered an investment opportunity involving patents and other IP. How solid are the patents? Sound enough to invest? How do you get beyond the glossy pitch to pressure-test the IP that sits at the heart of the business proposition? You'll need to ask Smart Questions. Smart Questions will help you to challenge the opportunity, examine the IP value proposition and ensure that there is clear line-of-sight from each patent to a downstream return on investment. After all, the value of many technology companies is principally a function of the perceived value and strength of its IP portfolio.

Institutional Research Office & Technology Commercialisation Staff

Working with inventors can be challenging and a lot of your time can be spent explaining the operation of the patent system and the legal and commercial requirements for successful patenting. Why not short-circuit some of that process? Instead of giving them generic answers, give them the Smart Questions and let the researchers bring their answers to you. By empowering the drivers of innovation, Smart Questions will save you time, deliver better quality disclosures and a higher level of engagement from research teams.

Business Advisors, Consultants & Lawyers

Do your clients need see a patent attorney? Is a patent the right way to protect their IP? How can you save your clients money by ensuring they are fully prepared before meeting with an attorney? Which attorney should you recommend to your client? Smart Questions will help you address these and many other challenges you'll face when dealing with IP questions from your clients. Using Smart Questions will help you to tease out the real needs of your client and a targeted referral to the right patent attorney will help cement your status as a trusted advisor.

Patent Attorneys

As a patent attorney, you'll be right across all the technical aspects of your client's IP portfolio, but many of your clients are not. Rather than spending hours asking each of your clients the same sets of questions to prepare them for the commercial and patenting choices ahead, why not make it easy by providing them with a comprehensive set of Smart Questions in advance? It empowers your clients to make the right decisions and frees up your time. When you ask the Smart Questions, your clients will appreciate the unexpected insights that these can provide.

How to use this book

This book is intended to be a catalyst for action, as well as a guide. We hope that the ideas and examples inspire you to act. So, do whatever you need to do to make this book useful. Go to our website and email colleagues the e-book summary. Use Post-it notes, write on it, rip it apart, or read it quickly in one sitting. Whatever works for you! We hope this becomes your most dog-eared book.

I already know the IP system ... OK, skip straight to the Questions

Perhaps you already have a thorough understanding of the patent system in general, as well as some of the specifically Australian twists. You may be familiar with the implications, benefits, trade-offs and risks of the IP process. If you like, you can skip straight on to Chapter 4 where the structure of the Smart Questions is explained. Chapters 1-3 won't go away – you can always come back later.

But before you go, please consider reading 'Getting Involved' at the back of the book and see how you could become part of the Smart Questions community.

Chapter

1

The Patent System

Just as ideas [are] the source of innovation, so is innovation the vital spark of all human change, improvement and progress.

Theodore Levitt (American economist & Harvard professor, 1925 – 2006)

What's the story?

THE idea behind the patent system is remarkably ancient and goes back to the early 1400's when glass-blowers in Venice first developed an informal system of monopolies.

Travelling glassmakers then spread the concept of patent monopolies throughout Europe. The earliest patent document that still exists is a patent awarded to John of Utynam in 1449. John was an accomplished Flemish glassmaker and had perfected a process for manufacturing coloured glass that was unknown in England at the time. King Henry VI obviously liked stained glass windows and he was keen to bring the skills and expertise of this master craftsman to England. He offered John a deal: if you come to work in England *and* you commit to teach your craft to our native glassmakers, then I will grant you a royal 20-year monopoly for the manufacture of stained glass by your process. John agreed and a royal patent was issued to him, protecting him from competition in return for sharing his secrets with the glassmakers of England.

Today's patent system still operates in a similar way and for the same purpose: to accelerate the exchange of new ideas.

What's the point?

The best ideas should be common property.

Seneca (Roman philosopher & statesman, 4BC – 65AD)

The point of the patent system is to drive innovation and promote progress by rewarding inventors for sharing their inventions with the world.

The patent system underpinned the Industrial Revolution and is central to the global economy today. Even back in 1788, the founding fathers of the United States of America recognised that a patent system was vital for the progress of the fledgling nation. Congress was explicitly instructed to: *"promote the progress of science and useful arts, by securing for limited times to authors and inventors the exclusive right to their respective writings and discoveries"* (**Constitution: Article I, Section 8**)

Strangely, there is much debate nowadays over the value of the IP system and whether patents are 'a good thing' or 'basically evil'. This book is not the place for discussing the merits and failings of the patent system, but what happens when there is no reward for sharing inventions is illustrated by the tragic story of the Chamberlen family secret.

The Chamberlens were a prominent family of obstetricians in 17th and 18th century England, passing their skill from father to son. Peter the Elder was the most famous, attending the wives of both King James I and King Charles I during childbirth. However, the Chamberlens were not just skilful; they also shared a fabulous secret. Around 1620, Peter the Elder had invented an instrument that allowed him to deliver babies safely when others could not. If babies arrived feet first or there were other complications during labour, it was likely that the baby, and often also the mother, would die in childbirth.

The secret instrument he had invented was the forceps. If a baby got stuck during childbirth, the forceps could be used to grab hold of the baby's head whilst it was still in the womb, so that the baby could be pulled out. The Chamberlens applied for a patent in the 1680s for 'secrets relating to midwifery', but their request was denied. The result for society at large was disastrous. Rather than sharing their invention with the world, the Chamberlens continued to keep their invention a strict secret, passing it only from father to son for five generations. The family went to extraordinary lengths to preserve their secret, including blindfolding women during childbirth and excluding all others, including midwives and relatives, from the birthing chamber.

After years of work I've finally perfected my invention!

But can you turn it into money in the bank?

However, few secrets last forever and the mysterious instrument was eventually revealed by a fellow surgeon in 1734, nearly 100 years, or four generations, after its invention. Immediately, others set about improving on the original design of the forceps and over time developed the instrument that is still in use today.

Why is this a tragic story? Between 1620 and 1734 in England alone, many thousands of women and children needlessly lost their lives, because this simple instrument was not available to other doctors of the age. Deprived of the opportunity to profit from their invention in other ways, the Chamberlens chose to keep the forceps a close family secret.

In fact, so closely was the secret held that for a further 100 years after it had been revealed, there was much speculation over who had actually invented the forceps. Only in 1813 did Peter the Elder eventually get the undisputed credit for his invention. During renovations of the Chamberlens' ancestral home a cache of obstetric instruments, including one of the original forceps, was found under a trapdoor in the attic. Peter the Elder had been dead for 182 years.

This tragic story illustrates many of the advantages that a patent system can provide for both inventors and the wider society.

Key Benefits of the Patent System:

Inventors receive an **incentive to invent** and **acknowledgment** for their contribution in their lifetime

Inventors can **profit** from their invention **without relying on secrecy** to maintain their monopoly

Inventions are made **available for all** to use (and become free to use after the monopoly period finishes)

Technology develops more rapidly, because others can start improving on new inventions right away, adding their ideas and insights and adapting existing technologies for new uses

---

Of course, the patent system is not the only way you can protect your ideas, inventions and the fruits of your ingenuity. You can make use of a wide range of formal and informal ways including trade marks, copyright, design rights, plant breeders' rights, domain names, etc. Whilst this book is about patents, we'll explore the use and suitability of some of these other options in Chapter 5.

So what's the deal?

The deal today is still pretty much the same as it was when John of Utynam was issued his patent back in 1449.

If you have made an *invention* that is *useful*, still *secret* and if the *government is interested* in making that invention more widely available to others, then you can obtain a 20-year monopoly to *exclude others* from practicing your invention in *that country*. That's the deal!

Let us comment briefly on the key points highlighted in italics. We'll look at each of these in more detail when we get to the Questions in Chapter 6:

Invention: only actual inventions qualify for patent protection. An invention is something that requires a leap of the imagination beyond the obvious, something that does not simply follow from everything that has gone before. Patents are intended to reward special and extraordinary contributions, not small advances. If others in your line of business, when thinking about the same problem, would likely come up with the same answer as you, then why should the patent office reward *you* with a monopoly?[2]

Useful: governments will award patents only for inventions that actually work and that have commercial or industrial applications. Patents are not available for purely aesthetic creations. These may be protectable in other ways, e.g. by copyright, design rights, trade marks, etc.

Secret: a key requirement for patenting is that your invention is still secret and only known to yourself (and any co-inventors). If you have already let the cat out of the bag or others have come up with the same idea as you, then it's not looking good. Remember, the core bargain is: you share a *Secret* in return for a *Monopoly*. If the idea is already out there, why should government grant *you* a belated monopoly when others already have legitimate access to your idea?

Government Interest: there are certain inventions that government does not wish to encourage or have published and so patent protection is not available for such inventions. For example, if you wanted to patent a more effective nuclear detonator or a suicide machine, most governments would object to granting patents for these on policy grounds. Natural phenomena, abstract ideas, principles of science (e.g. $E=mc^2$) and mere discoveries are also excluded from patenting so that the progress of science is not held up.

Exclude Others: a patent does not actually give you the right to practice the invention yourself. It only gives you the right to *prevent others* from practicing your invention. This is an important distinction. By analogy, owning a car does not automatically give you permission to drive it on the street. You still need a driver's licence, registration, insurance, etc. to do that. However, owning a car does give you the right to exclude others from taking it for a spin and you can take them to court for theft if they do so without your consent.

---

[2] Australia also has a second-tier patent process, the innovation patent. The process for this type of patent is simplified and does not require an inventive step. However, let's not confuse the story at this stage. We'll explain this specifically Australian system a bit later on.

Country: patents are granted by national governments. If you want a monopoly in Australia, you'll need to get an Australian patent. That patent will not provide any protection for your invention in China. You'll need a separate Chinese patent for that. Sometimes people talk loosely about a 'world patent': there is no such thing. Even when a company claims their invention is 'patented world-wide', all that usually means is that patent applications have been filed in many of the major economies around the world. Just ask them if they have patents in Morocco and Guatemala and you'll soon pop their bubble of worldwide patent protection.

In summary: if you have made a patentable invention that is still secret, the patent office in Australia will offer you a 20 year monopoly for that invention in return for making your secret available to everyone.

That's pretty much the deal!

Chapter

2

It's not all plain sailing…

My definition of an expert in any field is a person who knows enough about what's really going on to be scared.

P. J. Plauger (American software pioneer & entrepreneur, 1943 –)

EVEN though the aim of the patent system is simple and noble, the way it works is far from straightforward. Every inventor has horror stories to tell about red tape, strange terminology, seemingly random objections and the pressure of immoveable deadlines. The worst part is probably the cost of the process not just in terms of money, but also in time. All that grief and at the end there's not even an assured outcome. The statistics for Australian patent filings are sobering.

The average provisional patent application has only a 20% chance of survival

Ignoring overseas applications and innovation patents, between six and seven thousand provisional patent applications are filed in Australia every year (see graph, black bars). Of these, well over half are abandoned or re-filed within 12 months and never converted into complete applications. Whilst this removes some of the chaff, the attrition rate increases even further as the patent process becomes more expensive and more rigorous. Of all the complete applications filed (grey bars), only about 35% make it through to ultimately become granted Australian patents (white bars). The whole process takes between 2 to 6 years and the attrition rate from start to finish is in the order of 85%. In short, your average provisional application has less than a 1 in 5 chance of making it all the way through the process.[3] Those are scary odds!

Australian Patent Office Statistics 1999-2008[3]

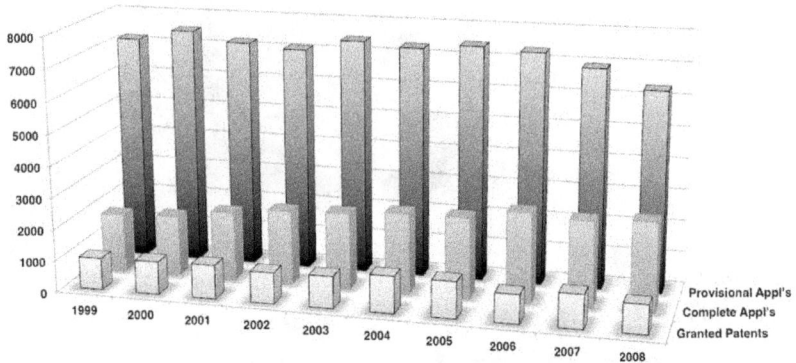

The secret to success is obvious: you need more than an *average* patent application – you need a *quality* application and a *sound strategy* to ensure you have an even chance of ending up with a granted patent. A few Smart Questions at the beginning can save you a whole lot of grief and expense later on.

What about commercial success?

Whilst securing a granted patent represents a significant win, it does not guarantee that the invention will go on to become a commercial success[4]. There are no statistics on how many granted patents ever repay their owner's patenting investment, never mind delivering a handsome profit. Our suspicion is that fewer than 25% of granted patents are genuinely profitable.

---

[3] The graph and statistics quoted are for patents filed and granted in Australia, where at least the first named inventor is resident in Australia. We have excluded innovation patents and patents filed in Australia by overseas inventors and corporations. The data were sourced from WIPO (World Intellectual Property Indicators, 2010) and IP Australia (Fact Sheet 4565 IPA update v3; IP Scorecard 2002-2006).

[4] See case study 4. for an example of some of the commercial challenges.

The only reliable data we could find in this area are from the annual survey of commercialisation activity in Australia's universities and public research organisations[5]. In 2007, the 77 organisations surveyed reported holding 11,237 pending and issued patents worldwide as well as 751 commercial agreements that made *some* money. Let's assume generously that each agreement covers a suite of five patent cases and actually makes a handsome profit, rather than just generating *some* money. That still leaves over 7,000 patent cases out there that are not even close to earning their keep. These are the statistics for a sector where inventors have access to dedicated commercialisation staff and expert patent and legal advice funded by their organisations. What about the thousands of independent inventors and SMEs looking to protect their new ideas with a view to striking it rich in the future? What are their odds of success?

Certainty of death, *small* chance of success... What are we waiting for?

Gimli in *The Lord of the Rings: Return of the King* (2003)

Clearly, the odds of securing a patent and striking it rich appear slim, yet the applications keep coming. Why? One likely reason the dropout rate is so high is because many inventors are chasing their dream without ever asking themselves some tough questions about the nature and true value of their invention up-front. People can get carried away with the excitement of their idea and rush into a patent filing without a clear picture of what they have and where they are headed. As a result, they get tangled up in the process, lose the plot, lose a lot of money and then end up as part of the statistics.

On the other hand, the right idea at the right time can have a huge impact and when that happens, protecting your innovations and inventions will return you a handsome profit.

If you are thinking of applying for a patent in Australia, you need to ask yourself a range of Smart Questions at every step of the process. Why? Because you'll need a lot of smart answers before committing your time and hard-earned cash to the process. What can you really protect? When is the right time to file? What kind

---

[5] National Survey of Research Commercialisation 2005–07 (July 09) Department of Innovation Industry Science and Research; Canberra.

of patent should you apply for? Who else can lay claim to your invention? The list goes on… Be prepared for every stage of the process. With smart answers and some good professional advice, you can shorten the odds of succeeding dramatically.

That is why we have written this book. It's to help you succeed.

Chapter

3

Ask the Smart Questions

If I have seen further it is by standing on the shoulders of giants

Isaac Newton (English mathematician, alchemist, astronomer & physicist, 1643 – 1727)

SMART Questions is about giving you valuable insights or "the Smarts". Normally these are only gained through years of painful and costly experience. Whether you already have a general understanding of the subject and need to take it to the next level or are starting from scratch, you need to make sure you ask the Smart Questions. We aim to short circuit that learning process, by providing the expertise of the 'giants' that Isaac Newton referred to.

Not all of the Smart Questions will necessarily be new or staggeringly insightful. The value you get from the information will clearly vary. It depends on your background, role and previous experience. Smart Questions will typically do one of the 3Rs.

The 3 Rs

Some of the questions will be in areas where you know all the answers so they will be **Reinforced** in your mind.

You may have forgotten some aspects of the subject, so the book will **Remind** you.

Other questions may **Reveal** new insights to you that you've never considered before.

How do you use Smart Questions?

The structure of the questions is set out in Chapter 4, and the questions are in Chapters 5 to 8. The questions are laid out in a series of structured and ordered tables with the questions in one column and the explanation of why it matters alongside. We've also provided a checkbox so that you can mark which questions are relevant to your particular situation.

How can I avoid getting bad answers?

That's a good question.

A quick scan down the first column in the list of questions should give you a general feel of where you are for each question versus the 3Rs.

At the highest level they are a sanity check or checklist of areas to consider. You can take them with you to meetings or use as the basis of your IP plan. Just one question may save you a whole heap of cash or heartache down the track.

In Chapter 9 we've bought some of the questions to life by illustrating a few of the common pitfalls with real-life examples.

We trust that you will discover a few real insights. There may be some 'aha' moments. Hopefully there won't be too many sickening, 'I wish we'd done that differently' moments. Even if you do find yourself in such a situation, the questions may help you to re-establish some order, take control and steer the project back into calmer waters.

Probably the most critical role of the Smart Questions is to reveal risks that you might not have considered. On the flip side, they should also open up your thinking to opportunities that hadn't yet occurred to you. Balancing the opportunities and the risks, and then agreeing what is realistically achievable is the key to formulating an effective IP strategy.

The questions could be used in your internal operational meetings to inform or at least prompt the debate. Alternatively they could shape the discussion you have with your co-inventors, commercial advisors, patent attorneys, investors, company management, research funders or the many other stakeholders involved in creating, protecting, prosecuting, managing and exploiting patents and IP.

In fact, it is our hope that many of the professional advisors in this space will hand this book to their clients as a first step to building more informed and more productive partnerships.

How to dig deeper

Need more information? Not convinced by the examples, or want ones that are more relevant to you specific situation? The Smart Questions website features a micro-site specifically for this book. This features a list of other supporting material and links to other websites or blogs. This is a fast-moving area.

Of course, there is also a growing community of people who've read the book and who are all at different levels of expertise. We encourage you to engage with us and with each other via the Smart Questions forum pages.

And finally...

Please remember that these questions are NOT intended to be a prescriptive list that must be followed slavishly from beginning to end. It is also inevitable that the list of questions is not exhaustive and that the law will change. However, we are confident that with the help of the community the list of Smart Questions will grow and continue to be refined.

If you want to rephrase a question to improve its context or have identified a question we've missed, then let us know so we can add to the collective knowledge in the next edition.

We also understand that not all of the questions will apply for all readers and to all businesses. However we do encourage you to read them all. There may well be a nugget of truth that can be adapted to your circumstances.

Above all, we hope this book provides a guide and pointers in areas that are of value to you, and that you experience many of the '3Rs' in the process.

Chapter

4

Patently Relevant Questions

Remember, nothing that's good works by itself, just to please you. You have to make the damn thing work.

Thomas A. Edison (American inventor & businessman, 1847 - 1931)

T HERE are over 130 Smart Questions in this book, but broadly speaking, they could all be summarised by five top-level questions. Everyone who is even beginning to think about a patent application should be able to address each of these five critical areas confidently. You need to ask yourself:

1. **What can I patent (and what are the alternatives)?**
2. I know what I have, but... **Do I have what it takes?**
3. Good news, but... **Should I patent my idea?**
4. Now choose... **What type of patent do I need?**
5. Everything is lined up, so... **How do I apply for one?**

Each of these five top-level Smart Questions is addressed in the following chapters. In each chapter you'll find more detailed sets of Smart Questions, which explore that topic. These are designed to help you arrive at smart answers tailored to your specific circumstances. Each section and sub-section deals with a specific topic, so feel free to dip into specific areas of interest or work through the questions top to bottom – whatever works for you.

Let us add one disclaimer though: the Smart Questions and associated explanations are intended as a guide to you, but should not be regarded as authoritative statements on the relevant law and procedure. They are not legal or patent advice. Whilst we have tried to ensure the information presented is accurate and up to date, we recommend that you discuss your specific circumstances with your patent attorney or other IP or legal advisor. You can also find more information and up-to-date web links at the Smart Questions micro-site for this book at *www.smart-questions.com*.

We also ***strongly*** recommend that you seek professional assistance before applying for a patent. Patent drafting in particular is a very technical skill. This is not a game for amateurs or the faint-hearted. If you don't believe us, skip straight to Chapter 9 and start this book by reading case study 5: What a difference a word makes...

To help you locate the Smart Questions of interest to you right now, here is a list of the chapters and sub-sections of the book. It's time to dive in and challenge yourself with a few Smart Questions about your favourite idea or invention.

Chapter 5: What can I protect and how?

1. **Section A** – What's the big idea and how can I protect it?
2. **Section B** – Why go for a patent and what are my options?

Chapter 6: Do I have what it takes?

1. **Section A** – Is my idea patentable, do I have the right to apply?
2. **Section B** – What might prevent me from getting a patent?

Chapter 7: Should I patent my idea?

1. **Section A** – How strong will my patent be?
2. **Section B** – Does it stack up commercially?
3. **Section C** – Timing is everything…?

Chapter 8: What type of patent is best and how do I apply for one?

1. **Section A** – What type of application is best?
2. **Section B** – How do I apply?
3. **Section C** – Finding the right patent attorney…

Chapter 9: Case Studies: when the rubber hits the road…

1. Kambrook - to patent or not to patent...
2. Benitec - inventorship, ownership and commercial opportunity...
3. Confidentiality Agreements – not quite…
4. Market opportunity ≠ market demand
5. What a difference a word makes…
6. Gray vs. UWA – IP ownership decided in the Federal Court
7. And now for something completely different

Chapter

5

What can I protect and how?

The vitality of thought is an adventure. Ideas won't keep. Something must be done about them.

Alfred North Whitehead (English mathematician, 1861 – 1947)

S OMETHING must be done about new ideas, but what exactly? Before you can begin to answer that question, you need to have a clear view of what you've actually invented and how you will convert that idea into your own pot of gold.

Once you are clear on your objective, you should ask yourself why you think a patent would be useful to you? One of the most common responses we hear is: "because I want to stop others from stealing my idea." Trying to keep your idea away from others is not perhaps the best reason for patenting, but many inventors start with that simple motivation.

Deciding to invest in a patent is a long-term commitment and should not be undertaken lightly. In this section, we'll invite you to clarify what *exactly* you have invented and explore the many ways in which a patent might benefit you and your venture. We'll also consider what other mechanisms might be available to protect your big idea.

We have grouped the questions in this chapter into two sections:

1. **Section A** – What's the big idea and how can I protect it?
2. **Section B** – Why go for a patent and what are my options?

The answers to those questions will help you to flesh out what you want to achieve by filing an Australian patent application and whether that's actually your best move.

5.1 What is the big idea and how can I protect it?

What exactly have you invented? This question seems so banal, yet many fledgling inventors struggle to answer that question clearly on the first attempt.

It's obvious, we've invented a better mousetrap, they say. Sometimes only after prolonged questioning, might it become apparent that what the inventors have *actually* invented is a clever mechanism for releasing the energy in a coiled spring much more forcefully. Being forensic about the nature of the invention can throw a whole new light on the invention itself. Could this invention be useful for springs in car suspensions? For watches? In high-performance catapults?

You've invented a new drug against cancer? There could be a number of actual inventions here: the drug itself, its use as a treatment for cancer (any other diseases?), the way to synthesise the drug, the way to administer it, knowledge of which chemical variants of the drug are active and which are inactive, etc.

Sometimes, inventors come to us with valuable intellectual property that's not actually an invention and needs to be protected in a different way. Maybe you've made an innovation and not an invention. How would you know?

Let's be clear what we're talking about. It's time for some Smart Questions...

☒	Question	Why this matters
☐	5.1.1 Is the idea a new mathematical method, a plan, scheme or other purely mental process?	If your invention is one of those it's game over for patenting, unless an expert attorney can craft a way around the fact that these items are specifically excluded from patenting. Other inventions specifically excluded from patenting include: human beings and biological processes for their creation, inventions that are contrary to law, inventions that are deemed 'inconvenient to the public' (whatever that may be) and artistic creations (for which other protections are available in copyright and design rights, etc.).
☐	5.1.2 Can discoveries, new abstract ideas, scientific principles or natural phenomena be patented?	As a general rule, discoveries of natural substances, natural laws or processes, etc. cannot be patented. However, where you have transformed the discovery into a useful process or have adapted it for another purpose, it is possible for a discovery to give rise to a patentable invention. A patentable invention needs to be a 'manner of manufacture', i.e. needs to be the result of human activity and needs to have commercial potential. This is a tricky area. Consult an expert.
☐	5.1.3 Is the invention a new thing, gadget or machinery?	Some of the strongest patent protection you can obtain is for what the experts call 'subject matter' patents – patents that cover a new piece of kit that has never been described before (like the forceps back in the 1620's). Subject matter patents are particularly effective because infringement is relatively easy to detect (hey - those clowns are selling the same thing!!!) and court orders are more easily obtained and enforced.

☒	Question	Why this matters
☐	5.1.4 Can a new chemical, a new substance, or a new combination of substances be protected the same way?	Patents on these kinds of inventions are also 'subject matter patents'. Mostly arising in the chemistry, industrial chemistry, biotechnology and related fields, these kinds of inventions often also include some 'methods' claims, describing how these new substances can be made and used, which can add an extra layer of protection.
☐	5.1.5 Is the idea a new manufacturing process or a new method of making or modifying something?	Sometimes, inventions are simply about a new, more effective way of making something. These *methods patents* are often regarded as less valuable than *subject matter patents*, because they are harder to police and enforce and more vulnerable to competitors finding another way to produce the same result. That said, there are plenty of methods patents out there that are worth millions.
☐	5.1.6 Can inventions that are methods for the diagnosis of disease or for treating humans or animals by surgery or other therapy be patented?	These kinds of methods are excluded from patentability in many countries, although the instruments, diagnostic kits and drugs themselves can be patented. *Methods* that serve medical purposes are tricky to patent in many countries because governments don't want to impede the practice of medicine with patent legislation. That said, a good patent attorney will work with you to craft patent claims that get you the right kind of cover.

☒	Question	Why this matters
☐	5.1.7 Can a new combination of existing technologies or a new way of using known methods or technologies be patented?	The combination of two existing technologies in a new way, providing this is innovative or inventive, can also give rise to patentable inventions, as does the application of existing technologies in new ways. A case in point is the drug thalidomide. It was abandoned as a sedative in the 60's because it caused birth defects when taken by pregnant mothers. Today, thalidomide has been re-discovered as an effective drug for the treatment of certain cancers. 'Use' patents are generally regarded as the weakest type of patent protection, because infringers are perfectly entitled to make, sell and use the existing technologies, just not in the way you've patented. The problem is, it's left to you to prove that they are actually using it for the specific purpose you have invented. Where such a process happens behind closed factory doors, that can be an impossible task and enforcing compliance can also be difficult. In some cases the 'users' are also your potential customers! That said, effectively policed, 'new use' and 'combination' patents can be a potent commercial lever.

☒	Question	Why this matters
☐	5.1.8 How can a new business method or a new way of doing business be protected?	Patents can protect business methods, although strict criteria apply. In general terms, the method has to be novel and inventive, as well as involving a technical solution or a technical advantage that is created through the interaction of a physical system or process with the business method. In other words, it can't just be an idea for a new scheme, there also has to be a physical system, perhaps an IT system, which is integral to performing aspects of the method. The law on business methods patents in Australia is fairly new and evolving, so it's vital to consult a patent attorney with expertise in this specialist area. Other countries take different approaches and in some you may not get any protection.
☐	5.1.9 Does the idea or invention involve novel and dedicated software in its operation?	Although the principal protection for software is through copyright (see Question 5.1.15), Australian patent law also allows patenting for certain software inventions, providing that the software itself is novel and inventive. To be patentable, the software must play a part in an industrial process or be directly applied to a business outcome. Many thousands of 'software' patents exist, but this is a complex and developing area of the law, so you're best to seek expert advice early.

☒	Question	Why this matters
☐	5.1.10 Does the invention have a distinctive brand name, logo, tagline or other feature?	Brand names, logos, expressions, sounds, smells and other distinctive marks that you use to identify your products cannot be patented. The way to protect these rights is through trade marks. Trade mark protection can be obtained by formally registering your mark as a trade mark '®', or simply through use (an 'unregistered' trade mark 'TM'). Trade marks are a subject matter deserving of a Smart Questions book all of its own (we're working on it!).
☐	5.1.11 Can a new design, a three-dimensional object or a two-dimensional pattern or ornamentation be patented if it's part of an invention?	You can't patent a design, including the shape, configuration, pattern and ornamentation by itself, although the good news is that creators of new designs can protect their unique appearance as a 'Registered Design'. To be eligible for protection, a design has to be distinctive and must not have been used or published prior to registration. Design rights are reserved for the visual appearance only and are **not** granted for functional aspects of products, the 'feel' of a product, what it is made from or how it works. Of course, there's nothing stopping you from applying for a patent on the functional aspects and a design right for the aesthetic aspects of your invention. In addition to applying for formal design rights, you may also have copyright protection in your design drawings, although the scope can be limited if you could have sought a registered design!

☒	Question	Why this matters
☐	5.1.12 Does the invention relate to a new plant variety?	In Australia you can protect new plant varieties in two ways: through patents for plants (in general and for specific varieties or cultivars), and by Plant Breeder's Rights (or PBRs) for specific plant cultivars only. However, you may also be able to apply for a separate patent for plant varieties generated through genetic engineering, for plant material, as well as for the processes used to produce it. In Australia a PBR and a patent may apply to the same plant variety, provided all the applicable eligibility criteria are met.
☐	5.1.13 Will the invention benefit from having its own internet address or domain name?	Domain names are managed independently of the patent, trade mark and other IP systems and can't be patented. Most public domain names are available to anyone on a first-come-first-served basis, although a few specifically Australian addresses like .com.au and .org.au are only available to resident companies and organisations. If a dedicated internet address is important for your invention, check early which domain names are still available and secure a number of the obvious variants for yourself. Domain names often tie in with trade marks, so consider investing in both early to cover your invention for every eventuality. Don't forget that greatidea.com, greatideas.com, great_idea.com and great-idea.com are all distinct addresses available to the first registrant.

☒	Question	Why this matters
☐	5.1.14 Does the idea involve or rely on specific know-how, trade secrets or confidential information?	Patent law requires you to disclose the best way of making and working your invention. This will require you to disclose any secret information and know-how. If such a disclosure would seriously disadvantage your business in other ways and if the invention cannot easily be reverse-engineered once in the marketplace, then perhaps maintaining the invention as a trade secret is a better option? The way the patent system is set up, you cannot patent trade secrets or confidential know-how **and** keep them secret at the same time.
☐	5.1.15 Is the creation a piece of software, a literary or artistic work, a musical work, a sound recording, film or a broadcast?	All of these creations automatically benefit from copyright protection, provided they are original. Although easy to obtain, in some ways the protection it offers is more limited. Copyright gives you the right to prevent others from copying your work – but does not protect the ideas expressed in your work. Other than in the case of software, copyright is likely to be the main form of protection available for such creations. As outlined above, software can also be patented if it's part of an industrial process or a broader invention, but in general, copyright works are not patentable.

☒	Question	Why this matters
☐	5.1.16 Does the invention involve a new design or layout for an integrated circuit or computer chip?	In Australia, the design or layout of integrated circuits are generally not patentable, but specific protection is available under the *Circuit Layouts Act 1989* (Cth). Protection is automatic, so no formal application is required, although you should document and clearly date your layouts in order to be able to assert your rights against others who copy your layout design down the track. Other countries have different rules, so if you want to protect a circuit layout overseas, consult an expert specialising in that area.
☐	5.1.17 How are the rights of authors and performers in their performances and written works protected?	Copyright legislation creates very specific 'performers rights' and 'moral rights', which are automatic legal rights belonging to the creators of certain works and which protect things such as the right to be attributed as the author or performer and rights of integrity in the works. You cannot protect these rights with a patent and they also cannot be transferred, assigned or sold! That said, authors and performers can agree to allow others to use their works in ways that would infringe these rights. This is always something to consider when asking another person to create a copyright work for you.

5.2 Why go for a patent and what are my options?

The journey of a thousand miles begins with a single step.

Lao-Tse (ancient Chinese philosopher & author of the Tao Te Ching)

What people forget is a journey to nowhere starts with a single step, too.

Chuck Palahniuk (American satirist and novelist, 1962 –)

The question 'Why do I want a patent?' is pretty simple. There are many reasons why people apply for patents – some good, some not so good. Some inventors we know file patents mostly for personal reasons. Others see the patent system purely as a means for financial gain, yet others want nothing more than to frustrate their competitors' product development plans. Whatever your objective, it's important to be clear about why you are embarking upon the journey before you set out and whether a patent is the best way to achieve that objective.

As soon as you've decided why you really want a patent, it's time to look at the different types of patent you can apply for: you can apply for an innovation patent, a standard Australian patent or go all the way and seek patents internationally. We'll go into more detail on this in Chapter 8, save to say that they all have their uses, their strengths and, of course, some drawbacks.

Let's explore some of the most common uses to which a patent can be put and which type of patent you might consider.

☒	Question	Why this matters
☐	5.2.1 Will a patent give me credibility and boost my career prospects?	Let's face it, being named as an inventor on a patent application is good for the ego. In many professions, it adds weight and credibility to a CV and many employers operate bonus schemes to reward staff for their inventiveness – which can fuel competition. Be careful to ensure that the lure of fame doesn't distort your grasp of reality. Patents are a primarily a commercial tool. Boosted ego, career prospects and professional credibility are poor (and expensive) reasons to file patent applications, although no doubt they can be a welcome by-product of the process.
☐	5.2.2 Will a patent protect my idea against others stealing it?	Unfortunately, the patent system won't help you there. The purpose of the patent system is to give others the opportunity to learn all about the advances you have made. In return, you get a time-limited monopoly. Of course, the monopoly exists only in countries where you have achieved a granted patent. Everywhere else, others are pretty much free to use your ideas. If keeping your invention confidential is vital, protecting it as a 'trade secret' may be a better option. Keep in mind though that keeping information secret is quite hard in the long run and strict secrecy can also limit your commercial success.

☒	Question	Why this matters
☐	5.2.3 Is filing a patent the best way to get recognition as the first to make my particular invention?	Being named as an inventor on a *granted* patent shows that an independent examiner has determined that you were the first to register that particular invention. However, you don't need to file a patent application and go through the expense of getting it granted to demonstrate that you were the first to invent something. If that is your goal, simply publishing your idea might be a cheaper and faster option. Many scientists prefer to publish their results and inventions without ever filing a patent application. Instead, they are seeking recognition for their contributions directly from their peers. Of course, publishing will mean that the idea is no longer secret and you will destroy your ability to seek patent protection for it at a later date.
☐	5.2.4 Can a patent help me to attract grant or investment funding?	Absolutely! In many areas, investors won't even consider your investment proposal if you have not protected the opportunity by applying for a patent – or better a clutch of solid patents. There are also plenty of business development grants (Federal & State) that are available to applicants who can demonstrate an appropriate under-standing of solid IP protection, of which patents form the primary part. Apart from providing a commercial edge for your business, a well-thought-out patent strategy signals to investors, banks and grant funders that you are serious and you know what you are doing. That said, not any patent will do. Serious investors will closely scrutinise the *quality* of your filing alongside the business case, so getting it right from the start is very important.

☒	Question	Why this matters
☐	5.2.5　Will a patent help my invention to become reality?	Good ideas nearly always require more development to get them from the drawing board to the marketplace. This will only happen if the person who is going to put in the effort (and the money!) can see scope for a reasonable return. If a competitor can simply copy a new invention the minute it hits the market, the scope to get that return is vastly diminished. Remember the deal? Having a patent gives you a limited monopoly in exchange for publishing your idea. It is the monopoly that will enable you to attract effort, money and resources to take your idea from its inception all the way to an actual product.
☐	5.2.6　How do multiple patents add value to my existing IP portfolio?	Patents are a bit like picket fences, putting a clear boundary around a piece of IP real estate that you control commercially. If you can secure 2, 3 or more adjacent blocks of land, it makes it much harder for competitors to muscle in on your turf and to 'invent around' your patent. A well constructed IP portfolio comprising patents, trade marks and other registered and unregistered rights is worth much more than the sum of its parts and adds attractiveness to prospective investors, licensees and buyers alike.

☒	Question	Why this matters
☐	5.2.7 Can patents be used to add 'bluff' value to my IP portfolio?	It's true, sometimes, applications are filed for their short-term 'bluff' value. Few people will admit it, but it does happen. The patent portfolio is looking a bit thin and you need to pad it out a bit for prospective investors? No problem. File a few more applications. Want to scare the competition with a forest of patents and overlapping IP rights that could be hard and costly to challenge one at a time? File a few more cases. These tactics might be effective short-term, but are costly and need to be used with great care as serious consequences can arise down the track, especially if the other side can prove fraud or bad faith. Tread carefully – this arena is not for the faint-hearted!
☐	5.2.8 Can a patent be useful to get access to other people's IP?	Often, companies holding patents still need additional licences from others to exploit their invention, as it relies on or utilises technologies patented by others. One way to access that technology would be to get a licence to use the technology and to pay royalties. If the other company also has an interest in your invention, another possibility may be to cross-license each other, so that both companies get to use each other's IP. We have seen companies deliberately file patents in their competitor's area not because they wanted to play there, but because they wanted to trade those patents for access to the other company's inventions in a different area. It's like a game of trumps, except here you can create your own super trump by being strategic. Of course, it all comes at a cost!

☒	Question	Why this matters
☐	5.2.9 Can a patent 'buy' me membership in a patent pool?	Many high-tech areas are so crowded with patents that the leading companies have formed patent pools around key technology areas. Members all pool their patent rights for other members to use in return for a proportion of royalties earned by all the patents in the pool. If you have come up with a key invention of interest to lots of players in a complex and inter-related technical field, then contributing your patent to any existing or proposed pool can be a cost-effective way to securing your place at the table.
☐	5.2.10 Can a patent help attract research and development funding?	A well-placed patent that is of commercial interest to others can get you access to some serious collaborative research money. Universities in particular use their patent portfolio to attract commercial sponsors who are interested in developing that IP with a view to perhaps later licensing it outright. This is an important use of patents. A word of warning though: the terms of the collaborative research agreement need to be drafted carefully as many inventors (and universities) have inadvertently 'given away' their valuable IP for a plate of beans in the guise of sponsored research funding. Even if you don't sell your IP at this early stage, some technologies can become so encumbered by pre-emptive and residual rights from sponsored research funding that they become impossible to commercialise later. Invest in advice from the best licensing expert you can afford.

☒	Question	Why this matters
☐	5.2.11 Why would I not just sell or license my invention to others?	This is probably the most common use for patents. If you don't have a patent, or some other form of IP, then you don't really have anything to sell or license. When you are licensing, you are basically giving others permission to use your patented invention in return for cash (or some other payment). You remain the owner of the IP and are generally responsible for maintaining it, enforcing it, paying the patent fees, etc. Where you sell (*legal-speak: "assign"*) your patent outright, the other party becomes the owner and generally the seller receives a one-off payment in return. Only the owner of a patent can stop others from using the invention. Licence and assignment agreements are fraught with pitfalls. If that is where you are heading, we strongly advise you consult an experienced licensing professional.
☐	5.2.12 Can a patent help me to stop others from exploiting my invention?	This is the pureblood purpose for filing a patent. Why would you file a patent for a fabbo-widget? Answer: because you want to be the only company in Australia selling fabbo-widgets (or fabbo-services) and are happy to sue the pants off anyone who even attempts to add a fabbo to their own widgets. Game on! After you've had your patent granted, consult a lawyer about your options to stop use by any infringers and the best way to be awarded 'damages' or 'accounts of profits'. (Remember: you can't sue people with a patent application. Your patent has to be granted first, although you may have rights dating back to when your patent application was first published). See also the section dealing with innovation patents in Chapter 8).

☒	Question	Why this matters
☐	5.2.13 I want a worldwide patent, don't I?	There's no such thing as a global or worldwide patent. Patents are granted by national governments and you'll have to choose where to apply for a patent. European governments have simplified the process somewhat, so that each patent is only examined once by a central examination authority, the European Patent Office (EPO). When approved by the EPO, you will still get a series of national certificates – one for each country you chose to patent your invention in. The key barrier to worldwide patent coverage is cost of seeking that protection. Chapter 8 covers some of the key questions you should ask to help choose where to apply.
☐	5.2.14 Is an Australian patent application relevant if my invention will be used mostly overseas?	The beauty of the Patent Cooperation Treaty (PCT) is that you can file an Australian patent application here, which can later become the basis for patent applications in 142 countries around the world. Those overseas patents will effectively be backdated to the date of your original Australian application. This gives you the advantage of managing the first few stages of the process relatively inexpensively in Australia before taking on the world. You can, of course, file your first application in another country and sometimes there may be good reasons for doing so, but this would usually be on specialist advice from your patent attorney. Some care is needed here, because a PCT application may still need to be filed and you need to do so through a country with which you have an appropriate connection. Also, not all countries are part of the PCT.

☒	Question	Why this matters
☐	5.2.15 Would an innovation patent be better than a standard patent?	You can think of the innovation patent system as patenting 'light'. Once examined and certified, innovation patents provide the same exclusive rights as standard patents, but only for 8 years from the date of application, not 20+. There are some other important limitations and the actual process (and cost) of having the patent drafted may not be all that much different to a standard patent. You'll find key questions to help you decide between the different patent paths in Chapter 8.

What else would you like to know about on this topic? Here's some room for questions. Please also share them with us!

Chapter

6

Do I have what it takes?

The best way to have a good idea is to have lots of ideas.

Linus Carl Pauling (Nobel Laureate chemist & activist, 1901 - 1994)

The difficulty lies, not in the new ideas, but in escaping from the old ones, which ramify into every corner of our minds.

John Maynard Keynes (British economist, 1883 – 1946)

YOUR invention may benefit from being protected by a patent, but do you have what it takes? Does your invention meet all the requirements for a successful patent? Actually owning all of the invention before you start filing patent applications is pretty handy too. Disputes arise regularly about IP ownership and these are not just about patents that are worth millions. You will also need stamina, fortitude, a budget and good professional advice. In earlier chapters, we have already mentioned some of the basic requirements for patentability, but it's worth exploring these key areas systematically. In our experience, many patent applications fail because of a failure to comply with one of the basic requirements. The advice of a skilled and experienced patent attorney is going to be essential in this regard. The questions here are designed to provide you with a starting point for those conversations and to alert you to some of the most common pitfalls. We have grouped the questions into two sections:

1. **Section A** – Is my idea patentable and do I have the right to apply?
2. **Section B** – What might prevent me from getting a patent?

6.1 Is my idea patentable & do I have the right to apply?

There are a number of strict criteria the patent office uses to decide whether you and your invention are eligible to receive a patent. This series of Smart Questions will provide you with a top-level guide to navigating these first hurdles. As always, these principles are intended as a starting point and you should seek the advice of a competent professional to advise you on your specific circumstances.

To be patentable in Australia your invention must be:

Not excluded from patenting (obviously!)

New and still secret

Inventive (standard patent) or innovative (innovation patent)

Commercially useful

We'll explore some of the finer points of these key criteria in this section. How does your invention stack up?

Of course, another key question is whether you have the right to be granted a patent. Anyone in the world who has had a bright idea can *apply* for an Australian patent, but only the rightful owner of an invention or innovation can be *granted* a patent. Who is the rightful owner of an invention? It is generally the inventor or someone to whom the inventor owes, or has given, the ownership of his/her invention (*Patent Speak: "Assigned title to the Invention"*). That someone could be another person, the company employing the inventor or perhaps a company commercialising the invention.

The situation gets more complicated where there are multiple inventors. Who was actually involved in the invention and who invented what? Who actually owns which part of the invention? What documents need to be signed by whom to tidy it all up? All of these can keep lawyers busy and in clover for months. That's before you decide how to actually take the invention forward and how much of the future spoils each inventor should receive for his or her contribution.

In our experience, when it comes to causing disputes and problems, ownership issues are second only to the tricky issue of how to divide the spoils.

Generally, the longer you leave it, the messier it gets and the more expensive it becomes to clear up. Ownership disputes and even just untidy ownership scenarios are likely to affect your ability to sell or licence your invention. The other party needs to be certain that their money has bought *all* of the required rights and not just 85% or even 99% of them. Case Study 2 is a classic example.

Keeping the ownership rights clear and transparent is essential and we have a few questions you should ask yourself early, to see how squeaky clean your invention is. Who owns your great new idea? Do you own all of 'your' invention? Have you got all the paperwork sorted to set you up for success?

☒	Question	Why this matters
☐	6.1.1 What exactly defines a 'great idea' as an 'invention'?	In chapter 5, we provided some examples of the types of things that might or might not constitute an 'invention' protectable by a patent. Interestingly, the way Australian law currently defines a patentable invention may be about to change. In a report published on 16 Feb 2011, the Advisory Council on Intellectual Property (ACIP) found that the current 'manner of manufacture' test for patentability was obscure, ambiguous and confusing. The current definition dates back to the old English Statute of Monopolies of 1623 and ACIP suggested bringing the official definition of a 'patentable invention' in line with current practice, as determined by the High Court in a number of recent cases. It is not yet clear whether the suggestions of the report will be implemented. Maybe in the next edition, we can offer you a clearer definition of a patentable Australian invention. In the meanwhile, the following questions will provide some guidance on the key principles and requirements for patentable inventions.

☒	Question	Why this matters
☐	6.1.2 How do I know if my invention is unique and new enough to get a patent?	This is a great question we wish more inventors would ask themselves before patenting. To be new and unique (*Patent Speak: "To Be Novel"*) is a key requirement for any patent. Before filing an application (in fact, before you spend too much time perfecting your idea!), it's worth searching existing patent databases, scientific literature, product brochures, the internet and other relevant sources for similar inventions. You should have a go yourself (see 'Sources of Further Information'), but the search for the same or similar technologies (*Patent Speak: "Novelty Search" or "Prior Art Search"*) is a bit of a black art and we strongly recommend you get a professional search done. At best, it will reassure you that there's nothing obvious out there that looks like your invention; at second best, it may tell you that your brilliant invention was first patented 30 years ago, so you can save yourself the trouble and money; at third best, studying 'similar' technologies might give you some ideas of where else your invention might be useful. Whichever way it goes, you will be better off after a professional novelty search. There are many and varied ways of searching, but time and effort spent early in searching is rarely wasted.
☐	6.1.3 What if my invention is unique but no longer new?	The standard against which the 'newness' of your invention will be judged includes anything you may have published yourself. Keeping your invention secret until filing a patent application is a key requirement for obtaining a patent. We discuss this further in the next section 'What might prevent me from getting a patent?'

☒	Question	Why this matters
☐	6.1.4 How do I tell if my idea is 'inventive' enough?	Australian patent law distinguishes between inventive and innovative ideas. If your idea is inventive, you can apply for a standard patent or an innovation patent, or both.
		In Australia, an invention requires a leap of the imagination beyond the obvious, something that does not simply follow from everything that has gone before. Your idea must not be obvious to someone with knowledge and experience in the technological field of the invention (*Patent Speak: "A Person Skilled in the Art"*). It must be something that this hypothetical person would not have come up with when faced with the same problem. This is the test applied to judge 'inventive step' and a key requirement for securing an Australian standard patent. Other countries have slightly different rules to judge if an invention is inventive enough.
☐	6.1.5 Is my idea 'innovative'?	An idea that provides an incremental advance, rather than a ground-breaking 'invention', could qualify as innovative. If your idea is innovative, you can apply for an innovation patent, but not a standard patent. In assessing 'innovative step', the patent office is looking for a difference between the innovation and what is already out there, where that difference must make a 'substantial contribution to the working of the innovation.' This lower inventive threshold forms the basis of the innovation patent.

☒	Question	Why this matters
☐	6.1.6 What sort of things can be inventive or innovative?	As you would expect, there are many inventive possibilities for how one might come up with something inventive or innovative enough to warrant patenting: • creating something unique and brand new • an unexpected new use for something already well known • a new combination of some things • a new modification of something • a new method of doing something • a new process of transforming or making things • a solution to a problem a lot of people have struggled with, even where that solution, with hindsight, seems obvious • the limit is your creativity… The questions in section 5.1 provide a good guide to some of the opportunities that may exist.
☐	6.1.7 Creating my invention seems a bit obvious to me. Is that a problem?	Many great inventions seem obvious with hindsight, particularly to their inventors. Obviousness is only a problem if your invention would have been obvious to others *before* you told them about your invention. One useful indicator that your invention is not obvious can be that others have tried and failed to come up with an effective solution to that problem. If your invention provides such a solution, by definition, it cannot have been obvious. Sometimes, the experts in the field are convinced that a particular approach will not work. Solving a problem using that approach would probably not be obvious. If in doubt, consult a patent attorney.

☒	Question	Why this matters
☐	6.1.8 Why does my invention have to have an 'industrial or commercial application'?	Patents are only available in Australia for inventions that are 'useful'. In Australia, this means simply that the invention needs to offer some material advantage and that the invention must deliver what the patent application claims it will do. Lack of a valid and substantial use (*Patent Speak: "Lack of Utility"*) is rarely a problem or a source of rejection by the Australian patent office. However, every once in a while, patent applicants try to claim something that's really a purely aesthetic creation or has no credible commercial application and will then be disappointed to see it rejected. Other countries have much more stringent 'usefulness' requirements and inventions may need to demonstrate worthwhile commercial or industrial applications to qualify as 'useful'. This can be important when thinking of applying for patents internationally.
☐	6.1.9 Who came up with the basic idea for the invention?	Was the Eureka moment entirely yours or did others contribute ideas, brainstorm with you to come up with the solution to the problem, suggest new features, etc.? It can be helpful to make a list of everyone and their specific contribution. In case of doubt, it can be worthwhile to consult an expert patent attorney to advise you.

☒	Question	Why this matters
☐	6.1.10 Who else could possibly claim to be involved with the invention?	Not everyone who has had a part in developing an invention is also an inventor, but it's best to be systematic and to keep accurate records of everyone involved with your invention and what their role and contribution has been. Contractors, designers, advisors, people you consulted, people who built the first prototype for you, the people who tested the prototype for you, everyone who's been in contact with your idea and invention… Make a list! Then show the list to a patent attorney to confirm who may be an inventor under the law and who was not. The list is also great for double-checking that you've got proper confidentiality agreements in place with everyone! Remember: no secret, no valid patent!
☐	6.1.11 Who owns any inventions I've made?	If you are the only inventor, the situation is relatively simple. If you have made the invention in your own time, using only your own resources, and where the invention is unrelated to your profession or employment, then the invention probably belongs to you. If you created the invention in the course of your employment, then your employer will generally own it. Employment contracts these days generally have IP ownership clauses and most will state that the employer, not the employee, will own any inventions made by employees as part of their employment. It pays to check your employment contract carefully (see Case Study 6.) and to consult a professional if in doubt. Of course, if someone else funded your work, you need to check the paperwork to see who will own what.

☒	Question	Why this matters
☐	6.1.12 I'm working at a university or other research organisation, so who owns my invention?	Before the now famous Gray vs. University of Western Australia case in 2008 (see Case Study 6.) there was some ambiguity. However, in the aftermath of the court case, most research organisations have revised their employment contracts to ensure that they own the inventions any of their employees make in the course of their work. The situation is somewhat different for students (undergraduate, PhD, MSc, etc.) who are not employed but whose stipend/grant is managed by a university. Who owns inventions made by students can depend on the terms of their funding agreement. Check the fine print, including terms of employment, awards, grant conditions and, of course, the organisation's IP Policy or Statute (usually found on the website of the University research office).

☒	Question	Why this matters
☐	6.1.13 Can I reclaim owner-ship of my invention from my employer or university?	Organisations with established IP policies generally regulate the procedures for IP management and commercialisation. Some will also provide for revenue sharing with inventors under the IP policy. Often, there are also provisions for returning IP to inventors under certain circumstances, so that inventors can commercialise the IP under their own steam. A classic case would be an invention in which the employer has no interest or does not wish to protect. Where this is a possibility, terms may involve a negotiated revenue share for the organisation if commercialisation of the invention is successful. Check your organisation's IP policy. If the policy doesn't deal with ownership by employees you can always have the discussion! Whichever applies, it is important to ensure any ownership transfer is in writing and is properly documented.
☐	6.1.14 What if I'm not the only inventor?	Then you need to work out who owns your part of the invention (see questions above) and who owns the other part(s). The more inventors are involved, the more difficult it can become to bring all of the parties together. The most convenient way to deal with that sort of complexity is for all inventors and IP owners to agree that one entity will own all of the IP and be responsible for managing it on behalf of the group. It is not necessary for this to happen and patents can be granted to multiple joint owners, although in that case you need to document very clearly and specifically the rights and obligations of all the stakeholders.

☒	Question	Why this matters
☐	6.1.15 If there are multiple inventors, do we need to decide the percentage ownership?	The whole notion of a specific share of ownership is common, but misguided. In law, even if one party is assigned only a 1% ownership share to the invention, they will enjoy exactly the same rights as the 99% 'owner'. What is commercially more important is who will pick up the costs, how decisions will be made and how the eventual profits will be divided. In order to give you the best possible chance of success, we suggest inventors and IP owners sign an agreement that brings all of the ownership rights together in one place (usually the party best equipped to commercialise the invention) and settle how decisions are made, who will pay for what and how the spoils are to be divided. That provides greater clarity from the start (lack of clarity decreases value!!) and will save you money and heartache later.
☐	6.1.16 Can a contractor own part of my invention?	Quite possibly. Many contractor agreements state that your money will buy you the work product – the thing they deliver to you – but not necessarily all of the intellectual property rights that attach to it. If the underlying IP is important, make sure that you get that written into the contract. If you don't, in the case of a contractor, the general rule is that the contractor will retain ownership, even though you might have certain rights to use it. It's a common issue, and it will definitely be a lot cheaper getting those rights at the beginning than trying to get them when the contractor can sniff a bigger payoff. Check the fine print!

☒	Question	Why this matters
☐	6.1.17 How can I ensure I own all of my invention?	Whenever you engage others to assist you in developing your invention, ensure that a confidentiality agreement and a written contract for the work are in place. The contract should specify that you will own all of the intellectual property arising from the work and that the consultant grants ownership of the intellectual property to you as part of the deal (*Patent Speak: "Assigns the IP"*). Ask a lawyer to help you with the detailed wording to ensure it's watertight. Remember, a confidentiality agreement usually won't be sufficient to 'assign' IP created by the recipient on its own, at least not without some serious wordsmithing!
☐	6.1.18 What do I need to do to transfer the ownership of IP to me (or to others)?	The transfer of intellectual property rights from one party to another is done using a legal agreement called an "Assignment". If you are an employee, your employer may ask you to sign a specific agreement assigning that particular invention to them. If you engage consultants, ensure you get assignment of their IP back to you (see the questions above). Patent offices around the world require proper assignment agreements to have been signed to ensure that everyone listed as the owner of a patent is legally entitled to that status.

6.2 What might prevent me from getting a patent?

In addition to the basic patentability requirements described in Section 6.1, there are a few other issues which regularly trip up prospective patentees. Some of these are effectively mandated by the patent office, but others are the direct result of carelessness on the part of the applicant and should be easy to avoid...

The most common pitfalls prior to filing a patent application are:

1. Premature disclosure or demonstration of the invention.
2. Premature partial disclosure of aspects of the invention.
3. Premature commercial use of the invention.

A number of other procedural problems can also prevent patents from being granted or cause them to be revoked. These include:

1. The invention is not described fully, described badly or so vaguely in the application that it would be impossible for others to re-create the invention.
2. The application is highly speculative, casting doubt on whether inventors have actually developed their idea beyond the 'thought experiment' stage and have some certainty that it will work in practice.
3. There is considerable doubt over whether the invention would work as described and achieve what the inventors say it will.
4. Naming people as inventors who should not be, or leaving out individuals who should.
5. The applicant is trying to claim more than one invention in a single patent application.

Have you thought about the following issues … ?

☒	Question	Why this matters
☐	6.2.1 How many people already know about the invention?	If the answer is more than one (yourself), you could be in trouble already, particularly if you have not yet filed a patent application and if you have shared your invention without formal confidentiality agreements. Prior disclosure by the inventors is one of the main killers of patents. As introduced in Chapter 1, if your invention is not new and secret, even if you yourself have disclosed it (*Patent Speak: "Your Invention lacks Novelty"*), you may not be granted a patent or run the risk of having it revoked down the track. Especially if your patent turns out to be valuable, it's not unheard of for companies to hire bounty hunters to try and dig up evidence of prior disclosure by the inventors – too often they succeed.
☐	6.2.2 How many others know about key aspects of the idea (even without knowing in detail how it works)?	Even disclosing a part of your invention may be problematic. Whilst you may have preserved the *novelty* of the invention, your disclosure may have put the inventive or the innovative step of your idea at risk (see Section 6.1 for details). All that's required to do the damage is to have given others sufficient clues so that they (or someone else in the technical field) could arrive at the same invention without too much further experimentation. In law, it doesn't matter whether you told your mother-in-law or the chief engineer of your competitor. Either disclosure could be equally damaging to proving that your invention still includes an *Inventive Step* (see Section 6.1).

☒	Question	Why this matters
☐	6.2.3 Who has been briefed on the invention in confidence?	Disclosure of your invention to an advisor acting for you under a professional duty of confidentiality, like a lawyer or patent attorney, is fine. If everyone else whom you have told about your idea has signed a formal confidentiality agreement, then you may be OK. That said, there have been cases where information has leaked out even though confidentiality agreements were in place. If that happens, there's little you can do and it's a risk you take with every agreement you sign! Even if no one blabs, sharing your secret idea 'confidentially' with too many people can be problematic. A secret known by 1000 people probably no longer qualifies as a secret, but what about 500? or 100? or 25? It's not entirely clear where a court may see the threshold, so be careful and deliberate with whom you share your secret!
☐	6.2.4 Is the idea sufficiently well developed to file a patent application now?	If you have disclosed the invention already, all may not be lost if you only need Australian coverage. Australia has a short 'grace period' of one year. Providing a complete patent application (as opposed to a provisional application) is filed within 12 months of disclosure of the idea, a disclosure by the inventor(s) is not counted against the patent. However, whilst it may protect you against your own disclosure, it does not protect you against others re-working or re-publishing your idea – that may still be a problem. Don't rely on the grace period except in case of dire emergency. Other countries do not recognise the Australian grace period and any prior disclosure would certainly put any international filings at risk. The golden rule remains: file first – share later!

☒	Question	Why this matters
☐	6.2.5 Is support from an investor or a commercial sponsor required before applying for a patent?	It is not un-common for inventors to seek financial support before filing a patent application. This is a dangerous move on two counts: disclosure can put the novelty of your invention at risk – confidentiality agreement or not (see above); and use of your invention commercially might also weaken your patent. Offering the invention for sale or investment could be construed as 'commercial dealing', i.e. the invention was in commercial use (to raise funds) before a patent application was filed. (*Patent Speak: "Prior Use Objection"*) Prior commercial use could be exploited as an argument to invalidate your patent down the track. Play it safe. File first, then seek support, but even then, be careful. There are a lot of sharks out there (see Case Study 3.)!
☐	6.2.6 Has the invention been used commercially or in a commercial setting before filing the application?	This is a tricky one. Use of a new invention for research and development purposes is, of course, permissible. However, if you (or others with your permission) have already been using the invention commercially, even in strict secrecy, the invention may no longer be patentable. Commercial use could also include demonstrating the product or trying to find a commercial partner before you've filed the application. Check with your attorney on where the boundaries lie and if you may be affected. Don't be tempted by the 'the patent office will never know' gambit. This is a poor defence: your competitors will know and a simple letter to the patent office with some evidence detailing your indiscretion can ensure that all your patenting efforts and costs were in vain. (*Patent Speak: "Prior Secret Use Objection"*)

☒	Question	Why this matters
☐	6.2.7 Am I prepared to put everything I know about the idea into the patent without keeping a few key tricks up my sleeve?	Patent law requires you to provide a clear and detailed description (including data and drawings, where appropriate) to show how your invention works and what is required to make it work. You also need to describe the best way known to you of making and using your invention. If you do not, your patent might be revoked down the track. The 'deal' is *full* disclosure in return for a commercial monopoly; so don't be tempted into sneaky business.
☐	6.2.8 Does the invention rely on a secret component or ingredients that can't be, or should not be, described?	To get a patent, you must disclose all the components that make the invention work. If you want to keep that magic ingredient secret, it may be better to keep the entire invention secret. Of course, sometimes inventions rely on components or complex biological extracts that are unique (leaf juice harvested from a particular tree on a Thursday night during a full moon) or other stuff that may be impossible to reproduce. In that case, you may need to deposit samples of the unique material to a repository so that others can access and analyse it if they wish to reproduce your invention. A patent attorney will tell you what is required.

☒	Question	Why this matters
☐	6.2.9 Is the invention fully developed to prototype stage?	Do you have to demonstrate that your invention actually works before filing? 'No'... and 'Yes'. It is quite possible to file a patent on a new invention before you've been able to build a prototype to test whether it will work as envisaged. The patent office itself will not test each invention to see if it actually works (although they can reject inventions which blatantly contravene the laws of physics). Many provisional patents are filed based on a great idea that 'should work'. By the time your patent comes up for completion 12 months later, you should be able to demonstrate that it actually 'does work' (*"Patent Speak: your invention is properly enabled"*). If you have filed 'on spec', you'd better have built at least a prototype or done other work so that you can substantiate the full extent of your claims to the examiner.

☒	Question	Why this matters
☐	6.2.10 Is everyone listed as an inventor on the patent application actually an inventor?	There is sometimes a temptation to reward the contributions of co-workers by making them co-inventors on the patent. This will put your patent at risk. Only individuals who have made an inventive contribution to the idea can be inventors. If you had the idea and just got someone else to build the prototype or carry out some experiments, that does not make them an inventor. However, if your co-worker provided additional suggestions and made improvements to your invention, then they might be. If in doubt, ask an experienced patent attorney for a review. Deliberately listing non-inventors on a patent risks invalidation, if challenged. If you want to acknowledge their (non-inventive) contribution to the success of the patent, why not give them some of the royalties? They'll probably like that more!
☐	6.2.11 Has someone's name been omitted from the list of inventors?	The patent office requires all inventors to be named on a patent – no exceptions. This is another area that's best sorted out right from the start, as legal challenges by slighted co-inventors (real or imagined) can soak-up lots of time, cash and goodwill, just when you are looking to commercialise the invention. If you accidentally or deliberately exclude someone, your patent may be held invalid. If someone made an inventive, but only a minor contribution, perhaps that can be reflected in the agreed revenue share?

☒	Question	Why this matters
☐	6.2.12 Does the patent application seek to protect two or more inventions in a single patent?	There is a general rule of one patent, one invention. If you have made multiple inventions, you should file a new patent application for each one. Commercially, that makes more sense too, although it will be more expensive. Your patent attorney will advise you.

What else would you like to know about on this topic? Here's some room for questions. Please also share them with us!

Chapter

7

Should I patent my idea?

If a man write a better book, preach a better sermon, or make a better mouse-trap than his neighbour, tho' he build his house in the woods, the world will make a beaten path to his door.

Ralph Waldo Emerson (American poet & author, 1803 – 1882)

WHILST Emerson's sentiment may still hold today, it's important to note that he was a poet and philosopher, not an inventor. In today's information economy, awash with new ideas and better mousetraps, just having a good idea is not sufficient. You need a hard-edged plan to market and commercialise your invention and solid IP protection *must* be part of that plan. There are good reasons to file patent applications, but there are also many good reasons not to (just yet). At the end of the day, patents are much like a fence to control access to a piece of 'intellectual real estate'. Whether it's worth building a patent fence will depend on many factors, the top six being:

- is the property attractive enough commercially to be worth fencing? (anyone keen on fencing the tidal swamp...)
- do you have the funds and stamina to fence all of the property properly? (a sturdy gate is of limited use without a decent fence around the rest of the property!)
- how strong a fence can you build (all fences have holes, how big are the holes in yours?)
- can you build multiple fence lines on the same property?
- can you patrol the fence against intruders?
- are you willing and able to throw out any fence jumpers?

Of course, this pre-supposes that you want to build a fence at all. Perhaps you are happy for everyone to graze their sheep on the paddock of your ideas. The modern term for this is 'Open Innovation'. That's perfectly fine, of course, but the risk you take in not looking after your property is that you may wake up one morning and find that your back yard has been turned into an open-cut mine and someone else is exploiting your ideas without even a thank you.

Some great inventions like the black box flight recorder, insect repellent and the powerboard (see Case Study 1.) have taken the Open Innovation route to market. Their inventors did not make a fortune from the fruits of their labours – others did. Open Innovation works well where lots of different ideas are required to develop a product, where making money is not that important to the inventors/contributors, or where the invention is relatively simple and cost-effective to make (e.g. software).

If your invention will take a long time to perfect and is costly to make, then even giving your invention away for free to everyone is no guarantee that it will be developed – quite the contrary. If someone else has to invest substantial funds to bring the product to the market, then they will want to be able to protect that investment against copycats. The classic example relates to pharmaceuticals. Industry estimates suggest that it takes around 1.3 billion dollars to bring a new drug to market these days.[6] Even if you presented industry with the recipe for a wonder drug, no one player would invest that kind of money to bring your drug to market unless it had solid IP protection. This is because, once approved, others could instantly copy the final product and make a tablet for a few cents that has taken you millions of dollars to develop.

So, quite paradoxically, if you want a complex invention to be widely available in the commercial marketplace, you must be able to offer a level of certainty that any investments in development and marketing can be protected against freeloaders. The best way to do that in most markets is through enforceable IP rights, particularly patents.

---

[6] *http://pharmalicensing.com/public/articles/view/1153412098_44bfac02291f1*

Of course, there are some industries where technology moves so quickly and market dynamics are such that the patenting process seems to move at a glacial pace by comparison. New media, information technology and telecommunications, for example, represent such fast-paced sectors. Other forms of IP protection may be more effective in those areas.

The only way to make good decisions is to make informed decisions. Plan what you are going to protect, how you are going to protect it, how you will commercialise your invention and how you will ensure that your turf is defended against infringers and copycats. Some of the following questions may help you decide which way to go.

We have grouped the questions into three sections:

1. **Section A** – How strong will my patent be?
2. **Section B** – Does it stack up commercially?
3. **Section C** – Timing is everything…

7.1 How strong will my patent be?

Assuming your invention has passed the basic patentability criteria (Chapter 6.) the next question is whether to go ahead with patenting or not. As a commercial tool, you'd ideally want your patent to be rock solid, impossible to get around, protecting a critical patch of 'real estate' and backed-up by lots of other forms of IP protection. Patents like that are pretty rare.

We've already mentioned in Section 5.1 that different types of inventions allow for inherently stronger patent protection than others. Unfortunately, you can't really control the nature of your invention – it is what it is. However, there are many other aspects that also contribute to the effectiveness of patents as a commercial tool. In this section, we'll invite you to explore the effectiveness of your idea in patenting terms, and what you might be able to do to strengthen your case. Perhaps it's worth delaying the filing of your patent application until some of that strengthening work can be completed? As always, when it comes to patent strategy, it's worth consulting someone who has professional experience to help guide your decisions in this arena.

To prepare you for that conversation, here are a few smart questions.

☒	Question	Why this matters
☐	7.1.1 Can the invention be easily and effectively protected as a trade secret?	If you can protect your invention long-term through keeping it secret, you may be better off not to disclose the secret to the world in a patent and you can save yourself a small fortune and trouble in the process. New manufacturing methods or recipes are more suited to this approach than gadgets or machinery. Think: as long as the Coca-Cola recipe remains a secret, no one can claim that they manufacture exactly the same drink. That said, secrets can be hard to keep long-term and others might stumble on your secret independently and might even seek to patent it themselves! It's a risk, but it may be worth taking.
☐	7.1.2 How well defined and worked out is the invention?	How small is the mesh of your fence? If your invention is very specific and can be described unambiguously, that will make for some strong patent claims. For example, a new type of ergonomic jam jar lid with 7-corners to allow easy opening by hand can be described very specifically, making for good solid patent claims. A claim to a plant extract with therapeutic properties would be less effective, unless the specific active ingredients, their combinations and the concentration ranges over which the ingredients are active could also be clearly defined. A patent attorney will advise you if more work would be advantageous to protect your invention more effectively.

☒	Question	Why this matters
☐	7.1.3 How broadly applicable is the invention?	Have you fenced all of the acreage where your invention might be useful? Where else might a new jam jar lid design be useful? On industrial drums? At the end of hand-tightened pipefittings? To operate large valves, taps and other machinery? Can you show other credible uses of your invention to make broader claims? A good patent attorney will advise you how best to claim your invention more broadly and what development work might be useful to support those broader claims.
☐	7.1.4 How difficult is it to create something that gets around the patent claims?	Every good idea will be copied or at least recreated – it's the highest form of flattery. One important way to reduce the damage this can do commercially is to make sure you end up with solid well worded claims in your patent application. Our advice is to resist offers for 'cheap' provisional filings, often prepared by a trainee or paralegal and not the primary patent attorney. Invest to get the best patent attorney you can afford onto the case from the start. When you get the first draft of your application back from your attorney, read the claims carefully and think about how you would try to get around the language used. If you can think around it, your competitors will! For a classic example, see Case Study 5.

☒	Question	Why this matters
☐	7.1.5 How similar is the invention to other ideas already out there?	Is your invention an improvement on something else? Has your invention been invented before? What (and who) else is out there? It's a good idea to do a patent search for similar kinds of technologies. You can do this yourself (see useful links at the end of the book), but we'd advise you to get a professional to sift the wheat from the chaff for you. With over 120,000 new patent applications being filed internationally every year, you'll be sure to find something in your field that's of interest. And what if, worst case, you find that someone else has already patented your brainchild a few years ago? Well, at least you can rest comfortably in the knowledge that you won't be spending tens of thousands of dollars chasing a dream.
☐	7.1.6 Is the invention dominated by, or does it infringe, other patents already out there?	Whoever markets and sells your invention needs to be clear about other patent rights out there and whether they may impact on their plans (*Patent Speak: to have "Freedom to Operate"*). That's another good reason to search for related patents early. You may find other patented technologies that already cover aspects of your invention. If that happens, you have a number of options including changing your design to stay clear of those areas, taking a licence to the other IP, or finding someone who already has a licence to the other IP to commercialise your patent. Of course, if your patent is hopelessly dominated by third-party IP, it may not be worth pursuing at all, but that's a call best made after consultation with an expert in the field and after careful study of the IP landscape around your idea.

☒	Question	Why this matters
☐	7.1.7 Does the invention require access to other patented IP to work properly?	Sometimes your patent may be hamstrung commercially even if you have complete Freedom to Operate. Imagine a revolutionary type of motor for use in high-speed centrifuges. In order to manufacture state-of-the art centrifuges yourself, you will need access to lots of other IP rights covering many aspects of modern centrifuge design. None of these affect your patent claims directly, but are still very relevant to any centrifuge you may want to build using your motor. In such an event, you could consider licensing your IP to an existing manufacturer, or you could look to in-license some of the other IP you need to sell the complete machine. The former route may mean that you miss out on the larger profits that come from sales of the complete product to the end user, but you benefit from the distribution network of the larger player. The latter will allow you to sell your own centrifuges, but you'll probably need to pay royalties to the other IP holders, increasing your costs.

☒	Question	Why this matters
☐	7.1.8 Is it reasonably possible to detect IP theft where it occurs?	The commercial value of a granted patent derives directly from the fact that you can sue people who infringe your IP rights. If the use of your IP rights is not easily apparent by looking at a competitor's product, how will you know when to enforce your rights? Imagine a patent covering a more efficient method of food processing involving a strict sequence of heating and cooling steps. It may be worth millions to the food industry, but how will you know that your IP is being infringed? Can you prove they followed your process and not a slightly different one behind their closed factory door? How valuable is this patent commercially if you can't enforce it? Among the strongest and most valuable patents are those where infringement detection is easy because use of the IP rights is apparent from the product itself.

What else would you like to know about on this topic? Here's some room for questions. Please also share them with us!

7.2 Does it stack up commercially?

The second prerequisite for a successful patent is that there is a viable commercial market for the idea. If there is no market or the market is hesitant to adopt the new technology then the commercial opportunity for your idea may not warrant the expense of patenting.

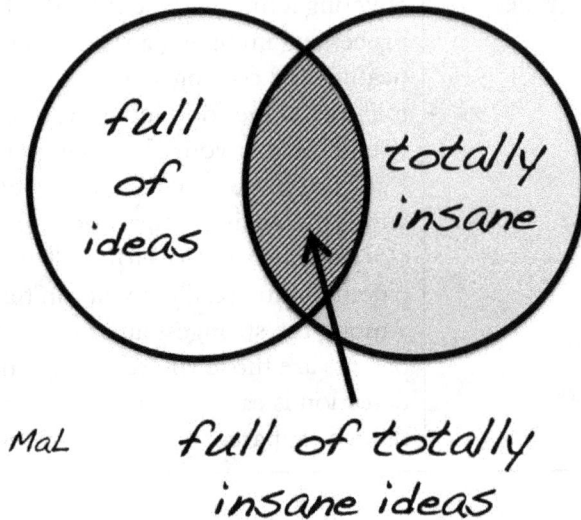

MaL

full of totally insane ideas

On the flip side, if you have developed a blockbuster 'have-to-have' product, then you can be pretty much guaranteed that others will copy your product, try to invent around it, challenge the validity of your patent in court and generally keep you spending money on lawyers until your ears start bleeding. That's when you need some strong and well heeled backers in your corner. A case in point is the 802.11 wireless LAN technology pioneered by the CSIRO and now incorporated into everything from phones, laptops, cameras, computers, cars and even some household appliances. It took a dedicated team of US lawyers and business managers from the CSIRO years of expensive lawsuits to finally enforce their patents. Of course, if your patent is commercially redundant, you are not likely to have those kinds of problems!

The following questions will start to explore some of the commercial landscape around your invention.

☒	Question	Why this matters
☐	7.2.1 How many different technologies already do what the invention achieves?	Does the world really need another solution in your area, another better mousetrap? How many are already out there competing in the marketplace? Beware of the: 'even if I can only sell to 1% of the US market...' fallacy. Yes, if you get just 1% of the US soft drinks business you will be a sqillionaire, but getting there is much harder than plugging numbers into a spreadsheet model. How much are your direct competitors selling? What is their share of the market? Be optimistic, but realistic, about the likely take-up rate of your invention. IP Australia's patent database lists over 400 patents relating to water sprinklers...
☐	7.2.2 What is the market opportunity?	Patents only make sense for inventions with a substantial market opportunity. Filing and prosecuting an Australian patent from first application to grant and paying maintenance fees for 20 years will cost between $20,000 and $30,000 for a fairly uncomplicated patent. Securing and maintaining a patent internationally could cost $200,000 to $500,000 and sometimes even more, depending on the number of countries. Do the sums: if your net profit margin is around 10%, you need to earn (sell) at least $250,000 of product just to pay for your Australian patent costs. How much market share do you need to gain to recoup your IP costs? Is your likely share of the total market opportunity big enough to cover your patent costs?

☒	Question	Why this matters
☐	7.2.3 How difficult is it to achieve the same end result as produced by the invention, but in a different way?	Unless there is a compelling motivation to adopt something new, you'll have a battle on your hands. If your invention allows people to do X more efficiently, how are they doing it now? How else might they achieve the same result in the future without using your invention? Think about your invention from the user's perspective. Is it worth changing procedures, scrapping existing devices and/or paying more for something new? What is the difference worth to the end user? Once you've factored in a decent profit margin for every link in the distribution chain, does the end user price still stack up?
☐	7.2.4 Will the market opportunity still be there by the time the patent is granted?	Patenting can be a slow process. On average, it takes 2 to 4 years to achieve grant of a standard Australian patent. In some industries, what's state of the art today is ancient history in four years' time. If your breakthrough idea can be integrated into products in a short time and is likely to be superseded in 3-4 years, you may be better off protecting your invention by other means, e.g. the innovation patent, trade marks or trade secret.
☐	7.2.5 Is first-to-market more important than market exclusivity?	In markets where technology is evolving rapidly and brand building is important, trade marks may be more valuable than the right to enforce a patent. Where all the energy needs to be spent on getting a product out as quickly as possible, the time and cost of the patent process may simply be too much of a distraction. A trade mark provides a means to build and protect value in your product's reputation, even when your competitors have matched the initial 'innovative' elements of your idea.

☒	Question	Why this matters
☐	7.2.6 How receptive is the target industry to new ideas?	Some inventions are clearly a quantum leap ahead of their time or solve a major problem. It does not always follow that the industry is actually interested in having that problem solved for them (see Case Study 4.). Many factors can conspire: it will cost them money (licensing fees, retooling, change, etc.); it may displace a profitable existing product; they may lose face (someone in a garage came up with a solution they've been seeking for years); and of course there's NIMBY – the 'not invented in my back yard' hurdle. That's not to say that patenting is not worthwhile if industry is not supportive, but be prepared for a long haul and make sure you have deep pockets, if that is the case.
☐	7.2.7 How prevalent is IP theft in the target industry and the main countries targeted?	In some industries, IP theft, misappropriation and infringement are rife, mostly because controls are slack and everyone is doing it. The same goes for some countries, although the list is slowly shrinking. If the main use of your invention is in an industry where respect for IP rights is low, you will need to take into account the cost of enforcement when you decide whether it's worth filing a patent. This is not about right and wrong, but our pragmatic view. If you, or a licensee of yours, are not prepared to enforce your IP rights, then the commercial value of your IP is pretty much neutralised.

☒	Question	Why this matters
☐	7.2.8 Is a granted patent sufficient to deter others in the market from infringement?	Who is your target audience? Will they respect a granted patent and voluntarily seek a licence or will they adopt a 'so sue me' attitude? A classic example of this was the recent series of lawsuits the CSIRO had to fight in the US against IT giants including Apple, Dell, Intel, HP, Netgear and others for infringement of its wireless technology patent. As a government agency, CSIRO had the backing and funds to sustain years of expensive litigation. If your patent is worth a fair fortune, expect to spend time in court defending it and bringing infringers to heel.
☐	7.2.9 Who is best placed to develop the invention to market readiness?	If your invention is ready for market 'as is' that's great. If your invention needs more development work, who can best do that work and who has the commercial reach and experience to then pass your technology on – value added? A key example is the pharmaceutical industry, where new experimental drugs often arise in university research labs, then get developed further by the biotech industry before being passed to the pharmaceutical industry to turn them into approved medicines that are marketed worldwide. No one partner in the chain is set-up to do the entire process. Who can you involve to assist you in developing and adding value to your IP?

☒	Question	Why this matters
☐	7.2.10 Who is best placed to exploit (manufacture, market and sell) the invention to generate a commercial return?	How your invention will ultimately be sold is an important driver of value. Some companies prefer to sell products themselves and keep all the profits. Others prefer to let others to do the hard work making, stocking, marketing and selling product and are happy to receive regular cheques in the mail for use of their IP. Between these extremes, there are many different business models, all with advantages and disadvantages. Before you file a patent, it's good to have a plan for what you'll do with the patent if and when you get it. Speak with an advisor about the different options of how you will ultimately turn your IP into cash.
☐	7.2.11 Who will assert the patent and enforce it against infringers where necessary?	The point of having a patent is to provide a commercial monopoly to someone for which they are prepared to pay a licence fee (or to enjoy that monopoly yourself, of course). The monopoly will only exist if others are prevented from infringing the IP rights. It follows that if infringers are not pursued, any genuine licensees are at a real disadvantage. Not only do they not enjoy the monopoly, they also have to pay licence fees that don't apply to the freeloaders. If your IP does not afford a commercial monopoly of any value, licensees will not pay for it. So, when you are planning your patent and commercial strategy, ensure that someone with sufficiently deep pockets and a sufficiently strong incentive is looking after your IP rights.

☒	Question	Why this matters
☐	7.2.12 Who will defend the patent against validity challenges?	When you start asserting your patent against infringers, be prepared to be counter-sued by them, claiming that your patent is invalid or not applicable to their product. Anyone monitoring the patent office publications can also make submissions to the patent offices directly, opposing your patent. If your patent is trivial, this is unlikely. However, if you are lucky enough to have the validity of your patent challenged by someone, this can signal that you have come up with something of value. Assuming the invention itself is sound, what you need then is an expertly crafted patent, a determination to see it through and a big chequebook. If your invention is any good, expect to have it challenged and plan accordingly from the start.
☐	7.2.13 What is the value of the invention to your or someone else's business?	It's important to talk about the value of an invention in the context of where and how it will be used. Does your invention shave a few dollars off the bottom line or open up an entirely new market? A new product among 100's may be worth a lot less to a major player than to a smaller company where that product has the ability to transform the nature of the business. The main value of your patent may be to strengthen the IP defences around the company's other patents or to allow them to sue a competitor. Maybe the company is looking to fundraise and only wants your IP to pretty up the patent portfolio. Value is relative and very much in the eye of the beholder. For whom is your IP going to be most valuable?

☒	Question	Why this matters
☐	7.2.14 Does the patent add value to a broader IP portfolio?	Sometimes it can be worth 'fencing the swamp'. The value of some patents may be not so much in the product monopoly they provide, but in the protection they give to other nearby patent estates. If you are a competitor, there is a big difference thinking about challenging a single isolated patent versus having to challenge a nest of related, interlocking patents, all of which are standing in the way of your planned product development. Somewhere, a cost-benefit decision needs to be made, whether litigation is cheaper (cost, uncertainty, time) than to negotiate a licence. The value of patents and other IP rights is generally enhanced if they are part of a well-constructed interrelated IP portfolio.
☐	7.2.15 Is it important to conceal from competitors what new developments you are working on?	The disclosure requirements of the patent system mean that at the very latest 18 months after filing a patent application, the world will know in great detail what you've been developing and where you're going with your technology. If it is important that technology development is kept under wraps for longer, it may be advantageous to keep the invention a trade secret for as long as is prudent during the development phase. The risk you run is that the secret will leak out or that you get scooped by someone filing their own application or publishing the same idea in the meantime. This is a risk you need to balance. An experienced IP attorney can advise you on this.

☒	Question	Why this matters
☐	7.2.16 Can the technology be developed to market readiness in a relatively short time?	Patents are traditionally valid for 20 years. Sometimes, product development timelines are so long that it takes most of the 20 years to get a product to market. For example, in 1998, UNSW and Qucor applied for the first patents protecting their ideas for a quantum computer. Today, these patents have only seven more years to run and it's unlikely that they will ever cover a finished product. The cost and effort was not wasted, of course. The early patents served to establish Qucor as a leader in the field and the company pulled in a lot of R&D funding on the back of them. Qucor also had in place a development and on-going patent filing strategy to see them through to market. Is your invention near enough to market that a product will enjoy a decent run of exclusivity over the 20-year life of the patent? If not, how else will the patent earn its keep?
☐	7.2.17 What other rights or permissions do you need to commercialise your invention?	A patent by itself may not be sufficient to allow you to market, sell or operate your invention commercially. Even a granted patent only gives you the right to stop others practicing your invention. To use your own invention commercially, you may well require other permissions, regulatory approvals, licences and consents. Do you know if you need any and how much they would cost, etc.? Any licensee of your invention will also need to figure these into its costings.

☒	Question	Why this matters
☐	7.2.18 Does the commercial opportunity outweigh the cost, time and risk of filing, maintaining and enforcing the patent?	This really is the key question, bringing together the answers of all of the subsets of questions in the first two sections of this Chapter. If it's worth doing, be prepared to invest, get the right advice and make sure you do it well. If it's borderline or not worth doing, then save your money and spend it on a great holiday with the family instead... or maybe invest it into developing your next great idea?

What else would you like to know about on this topic? Here's some room for questions. Please also share them with us!

7.3 Timing is everything...

The final aspect of the question 'should I patent my idea?' relates to the timing of filing a patent application. As with most questions relating to patenting, there's no one answer except for: 'it depends...' The one thing that is certain is that the right timing is critical for a number of reasons and getting it wrong can be fatal to your patenting aspirations.

If you jump the gun and go too early, you may not be able to describe and cover all of the opportunity your invention creates and it starts getting expensive too early. If you leave it too long, others may scoop you, the secret may leak out or time and commercial opportunity will overtake you. There is a whole range of factors to take into account.

One of the advantages of the modern patent system is that the costs, whilst expensive overall, are staged. They start out relatively small and then rise as you advance through the patent process. This staged process provides you with ready made decision points at which you can review your patent and the commercial opportunity it supports. If the idea isn't working out as planned, these natural break points give you an opportunity to 'opt out' rather than continue to invest more time, energy and money.

Of course, the process itself is very structured and the clock starts ticking the moment you file the application. So, when is the right time to kick-off the process? It's time for some smart questions to explore this.

☒	Question	Why this matters
☐	7.3.1 How long ago was the invention actually made?	In Australia, the priority date of your invention is the date on which you file your patent application. The priority date is important because your invention will be assessed against everything that was published prior to that date. If someone has a similar idea to yours and publishes that idea before you have filed your application, you may struggle to get a patent granted. Similarly, if you've invented something, but delay filing an application and someone else *later* makes the same invention but applies for a patent *before* you do (i.e. has an earlier priority date), then you will miss out. Slightly different rules currently apply in the USA, but with the *America Invents Act* signed into law by President Obama on 16 Sep 2011, the US system will shortly be brought into line with the rest of the world.
☐	7.3.2 Are sufficient funds and resources available to draft a quality patent application?	Many patent applications fail commercially because they are poorly drafted. If you are serious about your invention and it has commercial potential, then don't skimp on the one document that you want to be the foundation of your future wealth. Expect to invest between $5,000 and $8,000 for a good provisional patent application. Use an experienced attorney who is familiar with the field your invention is in. For more on finding the right attorney, see Section 8.3.

☒	Question	Why this matters
☐	7.3.3 How will the management and expense of the IP process be resourced?	Few patent applications find a commercial application or buyer within a year of filing, so be prepared to fund a decent provisional application *and* the costs to take the application to a complete or International application status a year later. The second step will probably cost another $2,000 to $4,000 if you choose to protect your invention in Australia only, or $8,000 to $14,000 if you want to protect your invention in a range of countries. After that, the process becomes steadily more expensive, depending on your choices – which is good, because otherwise it would be prohibitively expensive right from the start!
☐	7.3.4 Has the invention been disclosed recently?	If the invention has already been disclosed (we've already discussed the problems of early disclosure!), but the date of disclosure was less than a year ago, you may still be able to file a patent application in Australia and in some other countries, depending on how the disclosure came about. It is advisable to do so as quickly as possible, provided the invention stacks up commercially. You can't file a provisional application (see Section 8.1), but at least you have the opportunity to rescue some rights in Australia. Most other countries don't offer inventors a grace period, so if the invention has already been disclosed, you will not be entitled to a patent there. See your patent attorney quickly to check what rights you might have.

☒	Question	Why this matters
☐	7.3.5 How important is it to publicise the invention quickly?	Often in academic circles, there is great pressure to publish interesting results quickly, often before all the interesting ramifications can be explored. Of course, this can be at odds with the patent system that demands absolute secrecy *until* a fully detailed patent application is filed. This is an unhappy marriage and too many patents that are filed because the inventors want to publish end up falling over or being abandoned later on. If you are under pressure to publish an idea early, but there's not yet enough information to file a decent patent application, you'll need to decide what's more important and make a clear choice. Trying to have a bet each way is an expensive way to sit on the fence. That said, plenty of pre-eminent academics successfully manage the need to publish and patent. Planning ahead, and having a good relationship with a patent attorney who understands both needs will help.

☒	Question	Why this matters
☐	7.3.6 How developed and proven is the invention?	Ideally, at the time of filing your patent application, you will already have some proof that the invention works as described. The more data you can add to demonstrate the versatility and effectiveness of your invention (*Patent Speak: "Exemplifying the claims of your application"*), the stronger your patent will be. Where else might your invention be used? Speak with your attorney about what work you would need to do to show that your invention might be useful for other applications also (*Patent Speak: "Broadening the scope of your application"*). Both exemplification and broadening of scope will add value to your patent. Having an early conversation with an attorney can be useful, *before* the invention and all your development has been completed!
☐	7.3.7 How close is the competition to developing something similar?	If you are leading the field by a mile, you could consider broadening and strengthening the invention before filing. If the competition is hot on your heels, then it may be worth preparing to file quickly. Brief your attorney in advance, so they can start drafting the application in preparation for the final clinching piece of data. One of the classic patent races was the race to sequence the BRCA-2 breast cancer gene. Both Myriad Genetics and a UK charity consortium were running head-to-head. The UK team filed the day the first gene sequences came out of the sequencer and Myriad filed their patent application 25 days later with the complete sequence. The court battle lasted for years.

☒	Question	Why this matters
☐	7.3.8 How easy is it to keep the invention secret at this stage?	If it's easy to keep the invention under wraps and there's little risk of being scooped, you may have the opportunity of developing improvements and demonstrating additional uses for your invention before filing. These can all add to the value and strength of the application. If disclosure or testing of your invention in public is unavoidable during development, then you need to consider filing your patent application at an early stage. It's important to discuss your options with an experienced attorney.
☐	7.3.9 Are there important commercial reasons for patenting quickly?	If you want to be in the marketplace with a granted patent quickly, then the sooner you start the process, the sooner you will be able to enforce your rights. You can license your invention even before its patent application has been granted. If there is no commercial pressure to go fast, you may still choose to file, but take the slow road, which defers a lot of the heavy costs until later. Of course, sometimes patent applications are filed purely to be able to show third parties that "we're also in the game", to demonstrate innovative capability or to "pad out" the patents register before fundraising, etc. Many of these applications never make it through the process – they are not meant to. Their lifetime is only about 1-3 years. Think about what you wish to achieve commercially and proceed accordingly.

☒	Question	Why this matters
☐	7.3.10 How will the patent process deliver a solid return on investment?	Without a well worked out plan, it's easy to talk yourself into the commercial importance of doing something *now*. A patent is a business tool and you should have a business plan for every patent application you file. Work out how each patent will earn its keep. Part of that is an understanding of the likely cost and timing of expenses, which you can hopefully match against a reduction in commercial risk and a commercial return from your invention. If you are unsure about the commercial promise or how best to tap into the market, invest a thousand dollars or so in some expert advice before you sink $10,000 to $20,000 protecting a great idea without knowing where the financial return will come from.
☐	7.3.11 Do you have access to an experienced patent attorney?	Filing patent applications is both expensive and time-consuming. Navigating the process will require specialist skills and experience. Although IP Australia is making the process as easy as possible, particularly with innovation patents, getting advice from an expert remains essential. You may feel you can do some of these steps by yourself, but the way the patent system works, if you've made an error or have been advised poorly at the beginning, it may be impossible to recover your position. If you have not yet found an attorney you are comfortable with, then make finding one your next step (see Section 8.3).

☒	Question	Why this matters
☐	7.3.12 Do you have access to an experienced commercial advisor?	Patenting is, of course, only one half of the process. The other is all about turning that IP into value. Expert marketing, licensing and commercialisation can turn average patents into commercial success stories in the same way as inept commercial skills can ensure that the most brilliant ideas never see the light of day. Unless you are experienced in this area yourself, it pays to put a team together to assist you in making your invention successful. Some commercial advisors will structure their fees based on the success of the product. That way, they have a vested interest in helping you to make the invention as successful as it can be. You won't need a commercial advisor right from the start, but it's a good time to start looking. Beware of Cowboys.
☐	7.3.13 Is there a good time of year to file a patent?	Technically, it doesn't matter to the process at what time of the year a patent application is filed. That said, the patent process has very strict timelines, which generally fall into 12-month and 6-month patterns. Patent attorneys are human beings too and occasionally take holidays. The weeks before Christmas and early January are generally a nightmare and if you can avoid them, your attorney will be a) eternally grateful and b) able to give your application much more attention. Similarly, the weeks around June-July tend to be very busy, so if you can file your application in April-May or September-October, you may get more quality time from your attorney with lower fees (less night time work).

What else would you like to know about on this topic? Here's some room for questions. Please also share them with us!

Chapter

8

What type of patent is best and how do I apply for one?

To live is to choose. But to choose well, you must know who you are and what you stand for, where you want to go and why you want to get there.

Kofi Annan (Ghanaian diplomat & Nobel Laureate, 1938 –)

A USTRALIAN inventors are lucky. IP Australia offers creators of intellectual property more flexible options to protect their ideas than most other patent offices. Australia is one of a few countries that offer inventors a 'light' option in addition to the 'regular' patent process.

Under the standard process, inventors can file a provisional patent application as a precursor to a complete application, leading to a standard patent. Since 2001, inventors can also apply for a more limited type of patent known as an Innovation patent. This is an alternative to the standard patent. All patents provide exclusive rights, but there are important differences in the way the rights are obtained and how and when they can be enforced.

Apart from the length of exclusivity available, the main differentiator between standard patents and innovation patents is the level of inventiveness required. For a standard patent, the patent examiner will require your idea to be inventive and not obvious to someone who is also an expert in the field. This obviousness test does not apply to innovation patents. For these, you only require an innovative step – a lower threshold of inventiveness. The main differences between the three possible applications available to Australian inventors are summarised in the following table.

	Innovation application	Provisional application	Complete application
Intent	Innovation patent	Precursor to complete application	Standard patent
Inventiveness	Innovative	Inventive	Inventive
Claims	Max. 5	---	Unlimited
Priority date	Filing date	Filing date	Filing date or date of earliest provisional
Publication	Immediate	Not published	18 mths after priority date
Examination	On request	---	Compulsory
Granted	If basic formalities satisfied	---	After passing examination and opposition
Time to grant	Approx. 1 month	---	Approx. 2 to 4 years
Enforceable	Only after passing examination and once certified	---	After patent has been granted
Filing fees*	$150-180	$80-110	$340-$370
Examin. fees*	$400	---	$450
Annual fees*	$100-200	---	$250-1050
Lifetime	8 years from filing date	Must be 'completed' in 12 months	20 years from date of first application**

*Fees current June 2011. Additional fees may apply at different stages and attorney fees to draft the applications are not included.

**25 years for some pharmaceuticals.

Although an innovation patent is in many ways easier to obtain than a standard patent, any action to enforce it can be just as technical, complex and costly as for a standard patent. With this in mind it is just as important to seek appropriate advice when preparing an innovation patent application as it is for a provisional or standard patent application.

There are different paths available to obtain a standard 20-year patent. Inventors can file a standard patent application or choose to file a 'provisional' or an 'innovation' patent application first and then complete the application within 12 months. This will be slightly more expensive overall, but does defer some of the major expenses for a year. A provisional application is particularly useful, as it is not published and therefore gives inventors an extra year of secret development and tinkering time to beef up the data for the complete application.

If the invention also needs to be protected overseas, then inventors have further options. They can file a regular patent application directly with the overseas patent office (usually though an Australian patent attorney). Alternatively, any Australian provisional, standard or innovation patent application can be used as the starting point for applying for patent rights around the world. However, it is important to get both timing and strategy right. You should also be aware that, whilst an innovation patent can be the basis of a foreign patent application, it is likely the foreign patent office will apply a higher 'inventive' test for those applications. The rules for patenting are different in different countries and strict timelines apply. Patenting internationally is beyond the scope of this book, but whether at home or overseas, it is important to get the patenting strategy right.

Unfortunately, with choice come the need to choose and the possibility of getting it all horribly wrong. In this Chapter, you can explore the options through some smart questions. How you then translate your smart answers into strategy is best discussed with an experienced patent attorney.

We have grouped this chapter into three sections:

1. **Section A** – What type of application is best?
2. **Section B** – How do I apply?
3. **Section C** – Finding the right patent attorney...

8.1 What type of application is best?

Whilst the basic principles of innovation patents and standard patents are the same, each type is particularly suited to certain commercial situations. The following Smart Questions will help you to decide which patent is right for you and which application process best suits your needs and aspirations.

☒	Question	Why this matters
☐	8.1.1 Are sufficient funds available to invest in patent protection?	Each patent application is unique, but in very general terms, assuming there are no delays or oppositions, you can expect an innovation patent to cost between $2,000 and $5,000 to prepare and file with additional costs if you choose to have it examined early. A provisional application, including conversion into a complete application after 12 months, will probably cost around $8,000 to $10,000 with additional costs in examination, etc. thereafter. If you are patenting internationally, the sky is the limit as your fees depend on how many countries you go for and when. Your patent attorney will advise you.
☐	8.1.2 Is the idea inventive or innovative?	If your idea is 'inventive', it could qualify for protection by a standard patent as well as an innovation patent. If your idea is not 'inventive' but shows 'innovation', (see Section 6.1 for details), you won't qualify for a standard patent, but may still be able to apply successfully for an innovation patent to protect your idea.
☐	8.1.3 How well developed is the invention?	Innovation patents are published immediately, which can be disadvantageous if more development work lies ahead. Others might springboard off your work and get there ahead of you. If you want to start protecting your invention, but would like an extra 12 months to refine your approach or to build a prototype in secret, then a standard patent, starting with a provisional application, may be the better option.

☒	Question	Why this matters
☐	8.1.4 How close to market is the invention?	If you need patent protection quickly, an innovation patent can give you that coverage in a short period of time, even allowing for time to have the innovation examined and the patent certified so that you can legally enforce it against others. However, your protection will only last for 8 years. If it will take longer than a few years before your invention will be on the market, then the 20 year protection of a standard patent may be the better option. Alternatively, you could continue to develop your invention in secret and file an innovation patent just before launch, but you do then take the risk of being scooped. In some circumstances, you might even consider pursuing both simultaneously!
☐	8.1.5 Is maintaining secrecy for as long as possible commercially important?	Innovation patents are published pretty much immediately, disclosing all of your ideas to everyone. The detailed text of a provisional or standard patent application is not published for 18 months from first filing, so you can keep the details of your invention under wraps for longer using the regular patent process.
☐	8.1.6 Has the concept or idea already been disclosed by the inventors?	If you have already let the cat out of the bag, not all may be lost. Australia offers inventors a grace period of 12 months. However, if you need to rely on the grace period, you can no longer file a provisional patent application and must go straight to a complete or innovation patent application. Perhaps your disclosure has damaged the inventive step, but not the novelty of your invention. You may still qualify for an innovation patent. It's important you review any novelty and inventive step issues openly with your patent attorney.

☒	Question	Why this matters
☐	8.1.7 How long is the commercial life of the invention?	Some inventions are brilliant today and out-dated in two years' time. A standard patent will take at least 2 years to grant, by which time it might already be obsolete. In these cases, the innovation patent can provide much faster protection, although only for 8 years, so for products with relatively short commercial lives an innovation patent may provide completely adequate cover for your idea in Australia.
☐	8.1.8 How large is the commercial opportunity?	When you are protecting quite a substantial commercial opportunity, consider protecting it not just with one patent, but with a range of different patents. You could file a standard patent application on the core inventive idea of your technology and surround it with a series of innovation patents protecting some of the incremental advances and tweaks you've developed. This strategy provides powerful protection, but can get very expensive very quickly, so find an expert attorney to advise you on the right balance.
☐	8.1.9 Do you want to exploit your invention only within Australia?	If all you care about is your local Australian business and you don't care or don't want to bother with licensing your inventions internationally, then you won't need to worry about overseas patents. Either the innovation patent or a regular Australian patent will be just fine and if you change your mind within 12 months, your attorney can always file international applications at that stage.

☒	Question	Why this matters
☐	8.1.10 If you do want to protect your invention worldwide, where in the world is the main commercial opportunity for your invention?	If you have developed something that is only commercially relevant in Australia (perhaps a new way of controlling feral kangaroo populations) then an innovation patent or a standard Australian patent should do the trick quite nicely and you won't need to worry about international applications. Most overseas countries recognise the filing date of your first Australian patent application (innovation, provisional or complete) and will 'backdate' a complete application in their country to that date, providing you apply within 12 months from your first Australian filing date. That will give you time to decide whether to file overseas or not. If you do plan to exploit your invention overseas, you will need to speak with an attorney to decide how best to manage the local as well as the international application processes.
☐	8.1.11 Is short-term deterrence more important than long-term exclusivity?	The innovation patent can be a useful tool to build a thicket of closely related patents very quickly. Because they are relatively inexpensive to file, you could file two, three or maybe even more innovation patents on slightly different aspects of your invention. It may be advisable to also consider relying on a combination of standard and innovation patents to get the best of both types of patent protection.

☒	Question	Why this matters
☐	8.1.12 How quickly is an enforceable patent required?	If speed is of the essence, an innovation patent will come in handy, either alone or in combination with a standard patent. There may be many reasons why one might want to accelerate progress to a granted patent. The most common reasons are fundraising (investors generally value granted patents more highly than patent applications) or because your standard patent has not yet been granted and you want to act against someone infringing your claims (see below).
☐	8.1.13 Is your standard patent application still pending or delayed by opposition proceedings and someone is infringing your claims?	You cannot sue or injunct someone for patent infringement until your patent is granted. Because innovation patents can be obtained rapidly, speak with your patent attorney about dividing off an innovation patent from your original application. This type of patent strategy is beyond the scope of this book, but should allow you to commence infringement proceedings in a matter of months.

What else would you like to know about on this topic? Here's some room for questions. Please also share them with us!

8.2 How do I apply for a patent?

If you've come this far and are seriously thinking about applying for a patent, congratulations! Your chances of ending up with a granted patent that will not only look good on paper, but that will actually make you some money should be looking pretty good.

For the final two sections, we'll deviate from the Smart Questions format slightly in that there are fewer questions and more explanation up-front. This is because, once you have decided what kind of patent best suits your needs and which path to take to get there, the 'how to apply' step is then fairly straightforward and there are fewer choices to make.

If you choose to apply for a patent, *we strongly suggest you seek professional advice before deciding to lodge an application and use an attorney to draft your patent application.* This is because the commercial value of your patent stands and falls with the quality of the drafting and the way the patent claims are worded. Case study 5. provides a classic example of why this is important. What do you need to proceed?

Specification

The main body of any patent application is the written description of what you have invented. It must be a detailed and accurate description of the invention, how it works, including any alternative arrangements or other optional features and the best way known to you of operating and using the invention. It can also be helpful to list some of the already existing technologies and to distinguish clearly how your invention improves on these, how it is different or what known problem it solves. Even if you are using an attorney to draft the specification for you, it's helpful to prepare a detailed document yourself as a first draft. It will come in handy when you brief the attorney on the invention. You should also include diagrams or technical drawings as part of your application to illustrate the workings and features of your invention. Drawings and figures need to be in black & white (no photos) and are grouped together in a separate part of the specification. Check the format guide on the IP Australia website.

Abstract

Each specification should include a short paragraph summarising your invention. This should be written on a separate page at the end of the specification. The abstract is intended to inform readers about the key features of your invention. Abstracts are separately indexed by the patent database search engines and, providing you want your invention to be located easily, should contain likely key words in the text. "Horticultural fluid control and dosage device" is a lot less informative than "water sprinkler for lawns".

Claims

The claims of your patent determine and limit the scope of your protection. Therefore getting the claims right is absolutely critical! They are your most specific description of the key features of your invention and strict comparison with your claims will determine whether another product infringes your patent or not (See Case study 5. for an example). Your claims must define your invention and its novel technical features clearly to distinguish it from what is already known. The claims also have to relate clearly and reasonably to what you've written in the specification.

Filing an innovation patent application

The innovation patent application process has been designed to be as simple as possible. The IP Australia website has details about the required format for the specification text and drawings. You should also have a look at some relevant applications already on the database. Your application will need to include up to five claims that clearly state the scope of the patent rights you are looking for.

Although an innovation patent has a less onerous 'innovation' test, and is generally less complex to obtain, the claims are equally important and will also limit the protection you obtain. It is therefore very important that these are drafted correctly, and we suggest you seek professional assistance when doing so.

Other than the actual written description, claims and drawings, the only other requirement is to complete a patent request form (innovation patent) with your details and payment of the required fees. You can download the forms from the IP Australia website or complete it online, if you want to lodge the application by yourself. Providing the application meets the formal requirements for innovation patents, you should receive a notice of grant around 1 month later. That said, you can't enforce an innovation patent until it has been examined successfully and been certified, a process you can start straight away or leave until it's required. As for a standard patent, enforcement can be complex and costly, so think ahead and take appropriate advice.

Filing a provisional application

The process of filing a provisional application is similar to that for an innovation patent. You require an application form and a detailed written specification and drawings describing your invention. Because the provisional application itself will not be examined, you do not need to include a set of claims at this stage, although many attorneys prefer to include a draft set of claims. It can be helpful to do so, because thinking about the claims often helps to clarify the nature of the invention and the likely scope available. The final version of your patent claims is then required if you decide to complete the provisional application into a standard application down the track.

As soon as the provisional application documents have been submitted to IP Australia and the application fee has been paid, your provisional application is recorded and the priority date for your invention is locked in.

Remember that provisional applications have a strictly limited lifetime of 12 months. If they are not incorporated into a complete Australian application or into an international application within that time, the application will lapse and you will lose the priority date of your application.

This is a provisional proposal of marriage with the proviso that I may make a complete proposal within twelve months...

Are you an inventor ?

Filing a complete application

Often, a complete application derives from a provisional application and sometimes all that needs to be added is a set of claims. If you have refined your invention since filing the provisional application, you may also incorporate those refinements and developments, although if they are brand new insights or inventions in their own right, you may be better off filing an additional application. Your attorney will advise.

A complete application should include an application form, the complete specification (description, drawings & claims) and a Notice of Entitlement form confirming that you are entitled to apply for the patent. Of course, there is also a filing fee.

A standard patent application can have as many claims as you wish, but additional fees are payable down the track for each claim above 20.

Filing international applications

Filing patent applications internationally is beyond the scope of this book. Although most of the key principles apply in very similar ways in most other countries, there are also some significant differences. Considering this at the time of filing your initial application can be important, as the law or approach in your countries of interest may affect how you draft your application, particularly the claims you include. If your patenting ambitions go beyond Australia, your patent attorney will be best placed to guide you.

How well prepared are you to start the patenting process? Have you done your homework and are all your ducks lined up, ready to go?

☒	Question	Why this matters
☐	8.2.1 Are similar inventions listed in the patent databases?	Have you searched the patent database for similar inventions? Whether you are writing your patent specification yourself or are putting a document together to brief your attorney, have a look at what's already out there and the kind of technologies that other applications are referencing. You may discover other applications where your invention might be useful and can cite these as examples in your description. The patent system exists to help you build and improve on the work of others. Links to some of the free patent databases are listed in the back of the book.
☐	8.2.2 Who will draft the patent application?	Do you have the knowledge and experience to draft a patent application yourself? Unless you are experienced in how patents work and have successfully written your own, we strongly advise to consult a professional patent attorney to help you draft your final patent application. Drafting patents is a very technical skill, and the law can change quickly in this field. The need to understand the technical requirements of patent law are multiplied if you are looking to apply internationally.
☐	8.2.3 Is there a detailed description of your invention and the features that make it novel and inventive (or innovative)?	Even if you are not drafting your patent application yourself, you can save yourself money and time by preparing a detailed briefing document for your attorney. It will ensure he/she gets the invention right first time and that the attorney can get a good feel for the invention and present it in the application in the best possible light.

☒	Question	Why this matters
☐	8.2.4 Who are the rightful inventors of the invention?	Have all the inventors, if more than one, been identified? The often thorny issue of inventorship was the subject of questions back in Section 6.1. When filing a patent application, all inventors need to be listed and for innovation patents and complete applications, the inventors also need to complete a Notice of Entitlement.
☐	8.2.5 Are any of the inventors employed or in a job where they are expected to make inventions?	If inventors are employed by a company or working for a research organisation or university, it is likely that they will be bound by IP clauses in their employment agreement and need to manage their inventions according to the organisation's IP policy. It's worth finding out whether such a policy exists and what its terms are.
☐	8.2.6 Do the inventors have access to a specialist IP attorney or commercial development staff through their workplace, university, institution, etc.?	Most research organisations and universities have expert commercialisation staff on hand to assist their researchers with the protection and commercialisation of their inventions. Some even retain the services of dedicated patent attorneys. If you have the opportunity to make use of such 'free' resources, by all means do so. Of course, in such cases, the organisation often also has rights in the invention. However, if you are not confident that your invention is getting the best possible start in life, ask your organisation if they will hire an outside expert for you. You may need to chip in, but this will still be cheaper than going it alone.

☒	Question	Why this matters
☐	8.2.7 Have you chosen your preferred patent attorney?	Choosing the right patent attorney to draft your patent application is as important as choosing the right surgeon to operate on you if you need a heart bypass (ok, may be not quite as important...). Like surgeons, most patent attorneys specialise in certain technology fields. There are many different criteria for choosing an attorney and we are looking at some of the key areas in Section 8.3. Don't just take the first cab on the rank.
☐	8.2.8 How can Australian patent applications be submitted to IP Australia?	IP Australia has made the application process for patents relatively easy and you can lodge an application with IP Australia either by mail, in person, by fax or online. For up-to-date information on the IP Lodgement Points in each state and territory, the details for fax, post or online applications, etc. check the IP Australia website. The most convenient way is probably to draft the specification, save it as a pdf in separate files (specification, drawings, claims, etc.) and to lodge it online. You can also download the relevant application forms and declarations as well as pay the applicable fees online.

What type of patent is best and how do I apply for one? > How do I apply for a patent?

☒	Question	Why this matters
☐	8.2.9 Where else can I get help with the process?	There are many sources of assistance available to new inventors thinking about patenting. Your most reliable will be an expert patent attorney, but they will also be the most expensive. It pays to familiarise yourself with the basics, so that you can use their time most effectively. The IP Australia website is a great source of information on the patenting process, as are some of the State-sponsored business assistance websites. We have listed some of the main ones in the "Sources of further Information" pages at the end of the book. Inventor's chat rooms can also be useful for sharing information and war stories, but don't rely on internet forums or the net for an accurate interpretation of the law and process - they keep changing.

What else would you like to know about on this topic? Here's some room for questions. Please also share them with us!

8.3 Finding the right patent attorney…

"What every business owner needs is someone who is going to ask the tough questions. … The whole idea of a business advisor is having the comfort of knowing that there is someone on your team who's been there and done that."

Mark Bouris, Founder Yellow Brick Road (BRW April 2011, p22)

Finding the right patent attorney is an important part of the IP protection strategy and can sometimes feel like looking for a needle in a haystack. Of course, there are always competing interests, such as time, distance, money and other factors including expertise, track record, brand, resources, and back up. Most attorneys work as parts of larger firms, but don't lose sight of the fact that you are not hiring a firm. You are hiring an individual and their very specific expertise and, of course, personality. How you weigh these factors up is entirely a matter for you (and the other inventors and stakeholders).

In the final set of questions, we explore some of these factors and some tips to help you select a patent attorney that's right for you. The important thing is to make a choice you are happy with for the long run, because that's what the patent process is… a long run.

☒	Question	Why this matters
☐	8.3.1 How important is Location to you?	It would be great to find the perfect attorney right across the road, but that rarely happens unless your company has its own IP staff. However, the ability to communicate easily and, where necessary face to face, is an important consideration, particularly in the early stage as the applications are crafted and in the later stages when your attorney requires regular feedback to help argue the merits of your case with the patent office.
☐	8.3.2 How important is Time to you?	If you are very time constrained or do not wish to invest a lot of your own time into managing your IP affairs, make sure you appoint a very experienced attorney who can take care of your case without any unnecessary recourse to you. If you do not wish to become involved in the patenting process beyond the absolutely necessary, you could always retain a commercial advisor to instruct the attorney on your behalf and perhaps to sell or license your invention to a third party at an early stage.
☐	8.3.3 How important is Money to you?	Our view is that, if you believe in the commercial success of your invention, you should invest in the best possible IP protection you can afford. As with most things, you get what you pay for. If you ask for a provisional patent 'on the cheap', you will in all likelihood get a document that was written by a trainee patent attorney working in the firm, with minimal time spent by a more senior attorney. Always insist that the work is done by an experienced attorney or with the involvement of an experienced attorney, ideally a principal, partner or senior associate of the firm.

☒	Question	Why this matters
☐	8.3.4 How important is Experience to you?	This question is, of course, also related to money, but here is a rough guide to the seniority of the people you are dealing with based on decoding some of the titles you may encounter:

Patent scientist/technical specialist/trainee attorney: usually a scientist training to become a patent attorney, but not yet qualified as patent attorneys.

Patent attorney: usually a junior Australian patent attorney or an overseas-qualified attorney beginning to practice in Australia.

Associate: usually 4-6 years' experience.

Senior Associate: 6-10+ years' experience.

Principal / Partner: the top dogs in any law/patent firm, and therefore the most expensive! You should ask your attorney how they manage your work and who will be involved. There should be a balance between the cost effective use of resources and your need for experience and technical understanding. |

☒	Question	Why this matters
☐	8.3.5 How important is Expertise to you?	Experience is not the same as expertise, although both are important. If you can find an attorney who has filed a number of patent applications in areas similar to yours, you are also tapping into a vast pool of subject matter knowledge around your patenting area as well as, potentially, a network of relevant industry contacts when it comes to commercialisation. To find out about an attorney's technical expertise, ask for specific examples of similar technologies they have patented. If you have found a number of relevant patents on the database, look up the attorneys who managed those cases. Sometimes you can access years of valuable expertise in your area, paid for by others, simply by selecting the right attorney. Obviously large firms with many attorneys are more likely to have filed patents in your field, but many smaller firms or individuals also specialise in certain areas of technical expertise. The key is to do your homework and match your attorney as far as possible to the technical area of your invention.

X	Question	Why this matters
☐	8.3.6 How important is Independence to you?	The downside of finding an attorney who has great expertise in an area very close to your invention may be that he/she (or the firm more generally) is also looking after IP that may compete in the marketplace with yours. If there is an immediate conflict of interest, the attorney must tell you in advance, but sometimes conflicts only arise at a later date when someone infringes your patent and you want to sue. Most firms will have a 'conflicts' policy. If you think this might apply in your case, the best thing to do is to ask about your position. What you don't want to happen is to have to find another IP firm when it comes to enforcing your patent.
☐	8.3.7 How important is the Firm to you?	Some firms are known for their aggressive infringement prosecution, others are biotech experts, others specialise in local work for overseas clients, others combine several of these areas, etc. Most patent firms have a reputation and manage this together with their brand. If a particular brand is important to you, then selecting the right firm can be a great asset. Using a known firm with a good reputation may provide you credibility with potential partners, investors or licensees. You still need to make sure you get the right attorney, whatever the brand you choose. As in the supermarket, the bigger the brand, the more expensive the product tends to be.

☒	Question	Why this matters
☐	8.3.8 How important is Back-up to you?	The patent process is driven by tight deadlines. Particularly in the later stages of the process. We already mentioned that certain times of year are much busier for attorneys than others (Question 7.3.13). If your regular attorney was unavailable for a time, perhaps due to a lengthy court case, overseas trip or illness, is sufficiently expert back up available in the firm to look after your case? If not, how would your attorney look after your case in a crisis?
☐	8.3.9 How important is an Overseas Network to you?	Although in this book we have focused on Australia, when it comes to pursuing your patent portfolio overseas, it will be necessary for your Australian attorney to utilise patent attorneys overseas. Being able to access technically competent and experienced attorneys in a cost-effective manner will impact directly on the quality, and cost, of your protection. Discuss with your attorney how they will access and select such 'foreign associates'. You are looking for a range of established relationships which can be drawn upon to best service your interests, whether they be technical ability, reputation, location, cost or other factors.

☒	Question	Why this matters
☐	8.3.10 How important is Legal Support to you?	Patenting is only one aspect of looking after your invention. Some patent firms have their own legal teams to assist clients with the many specialist legal agreements that are required to license, assign or otherwise commercialise an invention. It is important that your lawyer works closely with you with and with your patent attorney to resolve any legal issues which might arise. If your preferred firm does have an in-house legal team, does that team have expertise in the way you want to commercialise your invention? If your preferred firm does not have the right in-house legal support, where will you access this?
☐	8.3.11 How important is Commercial Support to you?	Patent attorneys will look after your IP, lawyers will look after the legal agreements, but who can help you to look after the business side of your IP? Unless you are experienced in the commercial arena yourself, it pays dividends to work closely with someone who can help you to commercialise your invention. What's your marketing strategy? Who will you contact? How much should you sell for? What conditions should you attach? What's a fair royalty rate? All these are questions that can best be answered together with an experienced commercial advisor who takes the time to understand your business, what you want to achieve, helps you to define the best strategy to get there, and will then work with you every step of the way to help make your invention a success.

☒	Question	Why this matters
☐	8.3.12 How important is Personal Rapport to you?	The patent process is a long haul. You will be spending a fair amount of time with your attorney, your lawyers and your commercial advisor over the years. It's probably best to find someone you respect and with whom you get on well. That's not quite the same as someone who shares your enthusiasm for your invention. In fact, our suggestion would be to work with a team of people whose judgment you respect and who are not afraid to pressure-test your assumptions, to disagree with you and to be the devil's advocate. You will reap the benefits of their experience and probing down the track.

What else would you like to know about on this topic? Here's some room for questions. Please also share them with us!

Chapter

9

Case Studies: when the rubber hits the road

To invent an airplane is nothing. To build one is something.
But to fly is everything.

Otto Lilienthal (German aviation pioneer, 1848 – 1896)

In flying, the probability of survival is inversely proportional to
the angle of arrival.

Neil Armstrong (American aviator & astronaut, 1930 –)

WE have covered a lot of ground in the preceding chapters – not to put you off patenting, but hopefully to show you a few of the major pitfalls and to help you to navigate the complexity of the process. There are many great success stories where the patenting process has added tremendous value and underpinned the commercial performance of businesses great and small. You've read about them in the papers, so we won't talk about them here.

The road to success is often hard and, as in life, we learn more from our failures than we do from our successes. We'd like to share with you some real stories that were painful and costly for those involved. Why? Because it makes them all the more valuable for everyone else. The fact that a number of them are drawn from the world of big business should give you comfort that even experts in the field do occasionally get it wrong...

1. Kambrook – to patent or not to patent...

The tale of the power board has become a patenting legend[7]. The story goes back to 1972 when electrician Frank Bannigan invented the 4-way power board. His company, Kambrook, had been around since 1964, but at that stage was little more than Frank developing electrical appliances in his converted garage. It is said that he developed the power board out of pure frustration because his workshop did not have enough power points to test his products. The power board became Kambrook's first blockbuster product and soon his company was selling thousands of them worldwide. Kambrook became a household name.

Sadly, Frank did not patent the invention and it was not long before others copied the idea and the market was flooded with alternative models by his competitors. He is quoted as saying:

"I've probably lost millions of dollars in royalties alone. Whenever I go into a department store and see the wide range of power-boards on offer, it always comes back to haunt me." [8]

Hot on the heels of the power board came the plug-in electric timer and the plastic kettle (1977), all great Australian inventions that were not protected by patents – and quickly copied by others.

Kambrook has continued innovating, but now also invests into protecting its products and markets through patenting.

Kambrook managed to survive, even though it failed to protect its own markets in the early days. It survived because it was able to keep innovating and had a strong brand. Not all young ventures are so fortunate. It's probably prudent to try and make the most of your existing IP right from the start.

If you've got something worth protecting, protect it!

---

[7] *http://kambrook.com.au/about.html* (Apr. 2011)
[8] *http://www.ipaustralia.gov.au/strategies/case_kambrk.shtml* (Apr. 2011)

2. Benitec – inventorship, ownership and commercial opportunity...

Benitec is a small biotechnology company established in 1997. In July 2002, it joined the ASX with an impressive IP portfolio protecting a gene silencing technology set to revolutionise the diagnosis and treatment of disease as well as biological sciences generally. The company had big ambitions.

These were soon dampened, however, when the CSIRO called into question the rightful ownership of Benitec's IP. CSIRO asserted that the key scientists at Benitec had made the invention whilst still employed at the CSIRO and that the technology should therefore be properly owned by the CSIRO, not Benitec[9]. The CSIRO had also independently filed different patents on the same ground-breaking technology and their commercial plans were incompatible with Benitec's. The battle lines were drawn over who invented what, when, and who therefore had rights to what[10].

The dispute between CSIRO and Benitec lasted for years and was finally settled in December 2003[11]. However, for a critical period in the life of the technology, commercialisation by both sides was constrained by uncertainty over who would end up owning what.

Whilst all this was going on, Craig Mello and Andrew Fire, two Americans who had independently invented a related gene silencing technology, got on with the job of establishing their technology in the marketplace. Their technology took the market by storm and in 2006 they won the Nobel Prize in Physiology or Medicine "for their discovery of gene silencing by double-stranded RNA".

There's much to learn from this case: *most importantly, double check that you actually own every aspect of your invention. If in any doubt, sort uncertainties out early and amicably to avoid costly disputes later. When commercialising your IP, don't lose sight of the bigger picture. Time equals money and opportunity!*

---

[9] *www.lifescientist.com.au/article/89367/* and article/54486/
[10] *www.lifescientist.com.au/article/49192/*
[11] *www.lifescientist.com.au/article/40652/*

3. Confidentiality Agreements – not quite...

Not all confidentiality agreements are created equal. One so called 'standard' agreement we were shown included clauses that gave the industry partner ownership rights to any new ideas developed during the 'conversations' irrespective of whose idea it was. That's got nothing to do with confidentiality.

You haven't signed the Confidentiality Agreement

I have, but the non-disclosure clause prevents me from telling you where...

It also included a 'first and last right of refusal' clause. This would have compelled our client to check back with the company before he could do a deal with anyone else.

Make sure any confidentiality (or non-disclosure) agreement also includes a 'non-use' clause. An agreement not to share your secret with anyone is only half the bargain. The other half is an agreement not to make *use* of your invention and knowledge in their business. Permission should only extend to using the information for a specific purpose – generally to decide if both sides want to do business with each other or not.

One final warning – many inventors assume that the confidentiality agreement they signed with a technical collaborator or service provider for their initial discussions will also apply to the development (and ownership) of any new IP. It generally doesn't! You probably need another type of agreement to deal with that, including a written assignment of any new IP created.

IP and commercial clauses in contracts are important and there's no such thing as a 'standard' contract.

Ask an experienced IP lawyer for a confidentiality agreement you can use yourself. If the other side insists on using their contract, make sure you're comfortable and understand the implications of what you are signing and get professional assistance if you don't.

4. Market opportunity ≠ market demand

Just because you have invented a genuinely useful and brilliantly effective new device does not mean that it will be welcome in the marketplace. A spectacular example is the Environmental Safety Propeller invented by Colin Chamberlain (Australian Inventor of the Year 2009)[12]. On average, one person dies and 8 are horrifically injured in Australia every year by spinning propellers. In the US, the figures are around 30 dead and 200 severely injured. A typical three-bladed propeller inflicts about 160 impacts per second. One would think that any effective solution to this carnage would be welcomed by the market and industry alike – not so.

According to an industry expert, the American boating industry is actively hindering the marketing and sale of prop safety devices and lobbying against legislation to mandate safety devices on boats[13]. In August 2010, the US industry even managed to block a public education campaign by the US Coast Guard that included a video where drink and unsafe boating resulted in a prop strike. Having spent years promoting boating as a fun and safe activity, industry objected to the safety video because they felt it showed boating in a dangerous light. The industry insisted the Coast Guard return to promoting life jacket use instead. By November, the Coast Guard capitulated and withdrew the video 'pending further review'[14].

This is but one example to illustrate that just because you've come up with a genuinely brilliant idea does not mean that the world will be your oyster. Often, the more ground-breaking an invention is, the more vested interests it challenges and the harder it can be to find acceptance, never mind success, in the marketplace.

When thinking about the path to market, it's important to ensure you have the right connections and it can be advantageous to build and nurture these carefully from early on in the process. Gather feedback throughout, not just from those who support you and your invention, but particularly from those who oppose it or are critical of your approach. At worst, you'll learn what arguments will be levelled at you down the track.

---

[12] *www.abc.net.au/tv/newinventors/txt/s2736928.htm*
[13] *www.rbbi.com/pgic/prop-guard-inventors/prop-guard-inventors.htm*
[14] *www.rbbi.com/pgic/*

5. What a difference a word makes...

Many years ago, an Australian company filed a patent application for a new type of lawn sprinkler. The sprinkler used a series of shaped deflector plates to spray water in a variety of different patterns (circular, semi-circular, 90 degree sector, square, etc.). The plates were arranged on a circular disc so that the desired deflector could be moved into the water jet by simply rotating the disc – an ingenious design. In the patent claim below, 'fluid releasing device' means 'sprinkler', 'support' means the disc, and 'outlets' are the different deflector plates. The main claim of the patent read:

A fluid releasing device including: a base having an inlet, a support having two or more outlets and rotatably *mounted to the base, wherein each outlet can be brought into fluid communication with the inlet by* rotating *the support on the base.*

Not long after the release of this innovative product, a competitor started selling a sprinkler based on pretty much the same principle, but without rotating the spray deflectors (see image)[15]. The patent holder consulted their legal advisors about suing the competitor. Unfortunately, because the written claim only specified sprinklers where the plates are *rotated*, and the patent description suggested no alternative, an infringement suit would likely not succeed against a sprinkler with a sliding plate. The competitor had found a loophole in the drafting. If the original claim had talked about deflector plates *sliding* on the base, or simply specified *moving* on the base, then perhaps the patent would have been enforceable and thus more lucrative for the original inventors. What a difference a word makes!

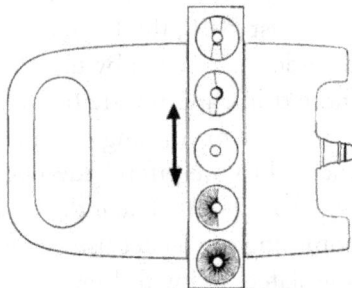

In Australia, particularly with the launch of the innovation patent, applying for a patent has become easier. Anyone can apply. However, the ultimate value of a patent rests on how well it is crafted and how effectively it can be enforced. In that regard, a single word can make all the difference. Speak to an experienced attorney about your invention to ensure you get it right from the start. If it's worth doing, it's worth doing well.

---

[15] We thank Robert Wulff for the image and the detail on this case.

6. Gray vs. UWA – IP ownership decided in the Federal Court

Until recently, universities had assumed that they had full ownership of any inventions made by the researchers they employed. The case of Dr. Bruce Gray shattered that status quo and underscored the importance of IP provisions in employment contracts generally.

Dr. Gray was Professor of Surgery at the University of Western Australia and was appointed "to teach, to conduct examinations" and "to undertake ... and generally stimulate research among the staff and students". Whilst working at UWA, Dr. Gray invented a microsphere technology for targeted cancer treatment. A series of patent applications were filed and later sold to Sirtex Medical Limited for development and commercialisation.

Dr. Gray's employment contract did not include explicit terms regarding the ownership of IP developed by him. Amongst other grounds, UWA claimed ownership on the basis that Dr. Gray was an employee of the university.

The Federal Court disagreed (Apr 2008) and the Full Federal Court confirmed this decision on appeal. Where University employees do not have a contractual duty to invent, and in the absence of explicit provisions for IP ownership in their employment contract, inventions made by university researchers were found to belong to the individual, not to their employer.

The Court emphasised that the university and public research environment is different from the private sector, suggesting that the outcome of the case could have been different if a private research organisation or a company had employed Dr. Gray.

Just because you invented it doesn't mean you own it! Following the Gray vs. UWA decision, many universities have beefed-up their employment contracts to ensure they own the IP developed by all of their employees. If you are dealing with public sector research organisations, ensure they have adequately addressed the IP ownership issues. If you are working with contractors to help you specify, design, build, modify, etc. your invention, be doubly sure any contract includes provisions for secrecy and that all the IP in their work passes to you on payment of the fee. As a sole inventor, check your employment contract to be sure that what you've invented is actually yours. If in doubt, seek professional advice!

7. And now for something completely different

And just when you thought you were never going to get a patent and that it was all too hard, here are some examples of granted patents and innovation patents which illustrate that amazing things do happen when dealing with patent offices around the world. The databases are full of amazing contraptions: some extraordinary, some visionary and some plain daft.

US patent 6,368,227 for a "method of swinging on a swing" was issued to Steven Olson of St Paul, Minnesota in 2002. Aged five, Steven could well be the world's youngest inventor with a granted patent. His dad Peter, a patent attorney, had promised Steven: "if you invent something, you can patent it." The boy had got bored with swinging backwards and forwards and discovered that he could swing sideways or in an oval pattern by alternately pulling the chain on either side. As the patent office could find no documentary evidence to show that sideways swinging had been practiced before, the examiner went on to issue the patent!

In 2001, John Keogh briefly achieved the impossible. He applied for, and was awarded, **Australian innovation patent 2001100012** for a "Circular transportation facilitation device" (a.k.a. the wheel). He said that he wanted to test the newly introduced innovation patent system, especially to see how closely innovation patent applications are vetted before they get the nod from the patent office. After some awkwardness for IP Australia, the patent has now been revoked, but can still be admired on the database.

Another classic is **US patent 6,329,919**, a business-method patent issued to IBM for an electronic queuing and reservation system for airplane toilets. This system takes queue barging to new heights.

US patent 6,805,607 titled "Scented doll with the appearance of an aged person" is looking to cash in on the ageing population. What is that smell? Smells just like Nanna... Lovely!

For sheer scope, you can't go past **UK application GB1426698**: Arthur Pedrick's 1974 invention of a cat-flap device able to recognise the coat-colour of his own cat to keep his neighbour's moggy out – and for use as a triggering device for a 1000 megaton earth-orbital peace-keeping nuclear bomb. Great work Arthur.

For other amazing patents, visit *www.delphion.com/gallery*, *www.patentlyabsurd.org.uk* or *www.patentoftheweek.com*.

Chapter

10

Final Word

At the present rate of progress, it is almost impossible to imagine any technical feat that cannot be achieved, if it can be achieved at all, within the next five hundred years.

Arthur C. Clarke (British sci-fi author & futurist, 1917 – 2008)

THIS confident statement from Arthur Clarke is almost the exact opposite of the much-quoted statement that *"Everything that can be invented has been invented"*, which is generally attributed to Charles H. Duell, Commissioner at the U.S. patent office in 1899. Mr. Duell's quote is almost certainly an urban myth, but the difference in sentiment is dramatic. In a space of a century or so, the horizons of mankind have broadened beyond the wildest imagination of the Victorian era. There were, of course, many factors that contributed to this, including two world wars and the cold war arms race. However, tremendous progress was also made in fields unrelated to global power struggles. Consumer products, therapeutics, manufacturing, engineering, energy technologies, IT, telecommunications, entertainment… the list is endless. Across the board, the patent system has underpinned the drive for technical, medical and commercial progress. Whilst not perfect, the patent system gives inventors the ability to profit from their ingenuity whilst, at the same time, sharing their inventions with the world. It is still the best system yet devised to facilitate 'Open Innovation'.

This book is about your participation in this tremendous information and ideas revolution. If you have a contribution to make, the world will be the better for it if you share your ideas. We hope this book will help you to decide whether patenting is the best way to go about protecting your interests and contributing to the store of knowledge and invention of mankind.

We know that patenting can be a daunting process and that the success rate is not high. However, you are now armed with some of the key questions, you know where to find good counsel, and we have introduced you to some of the flexibility that Australia's innovation system provides. With that knowledge, your odds of emerging at the end of the process with a commercially successful patent should be greatly improved.

We hope that your invention will one day become as celebrated as some of the other great Australian inventions like the bionic ear, the CPAP mask for sleep apnoea, wave piercing catamarans, polymer bank notes, the flu drug Relenza, the Gardasil cervical cancer vaccine, 802.11 Wi-Fi, Google Maps, or spray-on-skin for burns victims. Some of these have been developed in laboratories and research institutes, others were created in a garage. The most important ingredients are the creative spark and plenty of perseverance.

All the very best in your endeavours!

Matt & Philip

Sources of Further Information

To contact the authors, leave feedback, read about additional 'Smart Questions' that will be included in the next edition, and to access our up-to-date online links pages, please visit the micro-site for this book on the Smart Questions website at *www.smart-questions.com*.

Patent Office and Information Sites

IP Australia – the Australian patent office: *www.ipaustralia.gov.au*

World International Property Organisation – *www.wipo.int*

USPTO – the US patent & trade mark office – *www.uspto.gov*

Espacenet – the website of the European patent office – *www.epo.org*

Patents Online – *www.patentsonline.com.au*

Wikipedia – *www.wikipedia.org/wiki/Patent*

Industry Manuals on IP Management

Intellectual Property Manual for the Engineering Team (2009) Engineers Australia and Spruson & Ferguson

Biotechnology Intellectual Property Management Manual (2008) AusBiotech Ltd, the Victorian Government and Spruson & Ferguson

Intellectual Property Management: A Practical Guide for the Electrical and Electronics Related Industries (2007) AusIndustry, AEEMA and Spruson & Ferguson

All are available for download at *www.sprusons.com.au/ipresources.html*

Patent Searching

IP Australia – Australian Patent and Patent Application Search:
http://pericles.ipaustralia.gov.au/ols/auspat/#

World International Property Organisation PCT Patent Search:
http://www.wipo.int/pctdb/en/search-simp.jsp

USPTO – US Patent and Patent Application Search:
http://www.uspto.gov/patents/process/search/index.jsp

European Patent Search:
http://gb.espacenet.com/search97cgi/s97_cgi.exe?Action=FormGen&Templ
ate=gb/en/quick.hts

Relevant Organisations

The Institute of Patent and Trade Mark Attorneys of Australia –
www.ipta.com.au

Australian Institute for Commercialisation (AIC) – *www.ausicom.com*

Commercialisation Australia: – *www.commercialisationaustralia.gov.au*

Intellectual Property Society of Australia & New Zealand
(IPSANZ) – *www.ipsanz.com.au*

Inventors Association of Australia: – *www.inventors.asn.au*

Knowledge Commercialisation Australasia (KCA): – *www.kca.asn.au*

Licensing Executives Society of Australia & New Zealand
(LESANZ) – *www.lesanz.com/*

NSW Innovation Advisory Service: – *www.ausinvent.com*

Media and Business Information

Australian Anthill Magazine – *www.australiananthill.com*

Australian Design Unit – business and IP toolkit –
www.australiandesignunit.com/index.php/design/tool-kit/

NSW Small Business Toolkit – *http://toolkit.smallbiz.nsw.gov.au/*

Collections of Fun Patents

www.delphion.com/gallery

www.patentlyabsurd.org.uk

www.patentoftheweek.com

Getting Involved

The Smart Questions community

There may be questions that we should have asked but didn't. Or specific questions which may be relevant to your situation, but not everyone in general. Go to the website for the book and post the questions. You never know, they may make it into the next edition of the book. That is a key part of the Smart Questions Philosophy.

Send us your feedback

We love feedback. We prefer great reviews, but we'll accept anything that helps take the ideas further. We welcome your comments on this book.

We'd prefer email, as it's easy to answer and saves trees. If the ideas worked for you, we'd love to hear your success stories. Maybe we could turn them into 'Talking Heads'-style video or audio interviews on our website, so others can learn from you. That's one of the reasons why we wrote this book. So talk to us.

feedback@Smart-Questions.com

Got a book you need to write?

Maybe you are a domain expert with knowledge locked up inside you. You'd love to share it and there are people out there desperate for your insights. But you don't think you are an author and don't know where to start. Making it easy for you to write a book is part of the Smart Questions Philosophy.

Let us know about your book idea, and let's see if we can help you get your name in print.

potentialauthor@Smart-Questions.com

Notes pages

Notes pages